P9-DGZ-673

THE BEST PIZZA
IS MADE AT HOME

Donna Rathmell German

BRISTOL PUBLISHING ENTERPRISES, INC.
San Leandro, California

A Nitty Gritty® Cookbook

ISBN 1-55867-094-7

Cover design: Frank Paredes
Cover photography: John Benson
Food stylist: Suzanne Carreiro
Illustrator: James Balkovek

CONTENTS

Many thanks to all the people who ate the hundreds
of pizzas made and tested for this book. My family and I
had lots of fun entertaining friends and family
with all kinds of pizza doughs and toppings.

Thanks to Gary Webster, Wes Gillam, Steve Michaels and Chris Williams
who ate lots of pizza (and bread) for breakfast and lunch.

Thanks to Megan Pyle and Laura Wangsness
for all of their help in testing, tasting and computer work.

But most of all, thanks to my husband, Lee,
and to my daughters Rachel, Katie and Helen.

THE BEST PIZZA IS MADE AT HOME

Pizza is hot! In 1992 the pizza business accounted for more than $20 billion in sales in the U.S., and sales continue to increase.

Pizza has evolved into anything from a quick phone call for delivery of one of a common variety of commercially available pizzas to gourmet homemade pizzas with unique, tasty crusts and tantalizing toppings. Homemade pizzas are unsurpassed when it comes to freshness and quality. Pizza doughs themselves may range from a plain dough to one with several grains, flavored with lots of herbs and spices or fruits and vegetables. Toppings may be as simple as cheese or as complex as a delightful combination of sauce, vegetables and herbs. Sweet toppings are delicious for a breakfast or brunch pizza.

You probably have everything you need at home to make your own pizza, rather than depending on frozen pizzas or the local pizzeria. (See page 14, *Equipment*.) If you have a bread machine, a dough maker, a heavy-duty mixer or a food processor to make the dough, it is really a "snap." Your homemade pizzas can be quick, easy and delicious meals with much greater variety than you can find on any restaurant menu!

Occasionally pizza gets a "bum rap" when it is accused of being an unhealthy fast food, but one meal of pizza can represent all of the basic food groups: grains, vegetables, protein and dairy — and it can be as healthy or as loaded with fat and calories as you wish to make it!

A LITTLE HISTORY

There are many differing views about the historical origins of pizza. One school of thought is that pizza can be traced to the Persian Empire of 500 BC. Other sources indicate that the origins are traced to Egyptian flatbreads. Yet another theory is that pizza is traced to the Greeks and Romans. These theories are probably all true.

Breads, particularly flat breads, are used to this day as edible plates in many parts of the world. Ethiopians use teff flour (from an African cereal grass) to make injera, Mexicans use masa harina (corn flour soaked in lime juice) to make tortillas, and pitas are used in the Middle East.

It is obvious that the tomato-and-cheese-topped pizza common today could not have been traced to ancient times. Tomatoes are native to the Americas and were carried back to Europe by the Spanish explorers. Sometime during the 1700s, someone in Naples, Italy, first combined a flat bread pizza dough with tomatoes and cheese to make the first Neapolitan pizza. Pizza was introduced to the U.S. by Italian immigrants and the first pizzeria was opened in New York in the early 1900s. American soldiers returning from World War II began seeking out pizzas and pizzerias, which, in turn, thrust pizza into the mainstream American diet where it remains today.

———————

You will find recipes and ideas in this book for thin crust pizzas, deep dish pizzas, stuffed, rolled and layered pizzas — for sauces, toppings and fillings of nearly every description. Add your own ideas to the list: substitute your favorite herbs and spices. Use ingredients that you find in your refrigerator.

Have a pizza tonight!

INGREDIENTS

DOUGHS

Whether you use homemade versus commercially prepared pizza sauce or freshly grated cheese versus prepackaged grated cheese, there is nothing like a fresh, homemade dough. Select any of the wonderful doughs in this book to complement your favorite toppings. The dough may be as simple as a plain dough (such as you would buy at a store or pizza parlor, but much better) or may be a combination of different grains and herbs or spices. Following tradition, most pizza doughs are leavened with yeast, but baking powder may be used for a last minute dough if necessary. Substitute doughs and crusts you can also use:

- frozen bread dough
- packaged pizza crust mixes
- French rolls, halved
- tortillas
- English muffins
- biscuit dough (found in tubes in the dairy case)

- pastry dough (found in tubes in the dairy case)
- packaged flat breads
- commercial prebaked pizza crusts
- split or whole pita breads

SAUCES

There are any number of sauces available for purchase in grocery or gourmet stores. It is purely an individual choice whether you make your own sauce or use a commercially prepared sauce. A homemade pizza sauce is really nothing more than a few tomatoes (canned or fresh) which are seeded and chopped with some herbs to your taste. If you do elect to make your own sauce, double or triple the recipe and then freeze or refrigerate in small, pizza-size portions for quick and easy use.

I have never really measured how much sauce I use, but just go by the appearance. In fact, when I started working on this book, I went into national pizza parlors to discuss how they made their pizzas. When asked how much sauce they used per pizza, one manager gave me a very exasperated look and said "A ladle or so — just whatever looks right!" To prevent a soggy crust, spoon on only enough sauce to cover the dough, leaving a 1/2-inch border around the rim. If you prefer more sauce, you should brush a teaspoon or two of olive oil on the crust prior to spreading the sauce, which will help seal the dough and prevent sogginess.

Various sauces which may be used on pizza include:

- pizza sauce (tomato sauce with seasonings)
- barbecue sauce
- pesto
- a light brushing of olive oil only
- cocktail sauce
- ricotta cheese in place of sauce

CHEESES

There are many people who use a whole pound of cheese (4 cups) on a single 15-inch pizza. I, however, do not recommend using more than ½ pound (2 cups) of cheese on any single, 15-inch thin crust pizza. When layering the cheese on the pizza, make sure to place most of the cheese towards the outer rim of the pie, as it gravitates towards the middle when baking. If your pizza crust is soggy and tends to collapse when you hold it, chances are you are either using too much cheese and/or other toppings or you are layering the ingredients too heavily in the center.

Most of the recipes in this book call for 1 to 2 cups of grated mozzarella cheese for simplicity. I strongly recommend experimenting with cheeses to suit your taste. A 50/50 split of mozzarella and Monterey Jack is recommended as is a three-way split of mozzarella, Monterey Jack and provolone or a three-way split of a little cheddar with a combination of mozzarella and Monterey Jack. We hosted one pizza party in which everyone was asked to bring a grated cheese for pizza. Everyone chose their own cheese topping, no one pizza was alike and everyone happily tried all kinds of variations. Don't be limited by the following list — just about any cheese will complement a pizza.

- *mozzarella* (from half to all the cheese) is most common with pizza. It melts nicely. Prepackaged grated mozzarella is drier than that which you grate yourself and may brown or burn. Keep an eye on the pizza as it is cooking.

- *Monterey Jack* (up to ½ the cheese) also melts nicely and is often used in combination with mozzarella. For spicy pizzas, try the Jack with jalapeños.

- *Parmesan* (up to ¼ the cheese) is a very hard cheese and may now be found whole or "freshly" grated in the refrigerated section of many grocery stores. It is generally used in small amounts with other cheeses.

- *provolone* (up to ½ the cheese) is normally used with mozzarella or with mozzarella and Jack cheeses. It can also be used alone.

- *ricotta* (up to ½ the cheese) is wonderful spread directly over the pizza dough or it may be used as a base for stuffed pizzas and calzones.

- *Romano* (about ¼ the cheese) is similar to Parmesan cheese.
- *cheddar* (about ¼ the cheese) melts well but should be used with mozzarella. Too much cheddar may cause the pizza to be oily and the crust to become soggy.
- *Edam* (about ¼ the cheese), similar to Gouda, has a mild, buttery flavor which combines nicely with most cheeses.
- *feta* (about ¼ the cheese) is usually made from goat's milk and is associated with Greek and Middle Eastern flavors. It is easily crumbled over any pizza (2 oz. equals about ½ cup).
- *farmers cheese* (up to ½ the cheese) melts nicely and has a nice creamy taste and texture.
- *goat cheese* (about ¼ the cheese) melts nicely and has a strong flavor.
- *blue-veined cheeses* (up to ¼ the cheese), including Roquefort and Gorgonzola, melt nicely and have a strong, sharp flavor.

VEGETABLES

Almost any vegetable may be used as a topping on pizza. Most vegetables do not require any steaming or sautéing; however, vegetables such as broccoli, eggplant and mushrooms may be cooked first. Although I usually say *diced* or *sliced* in my recipes, vegetables may be cut julienne-style (into thin matchstick strips), cut on the diagonal, or otherwise cut into attractive shapes for pretty presentations.

- sliced fresh tomatoes, seeded. I like Italian plum or Roma tomatoes sliced into quarters or diced when using fresh tomatoes on pizza. To seed, simply slice off top of tomato and squeeze out juice and seeds.
- sun-dried tomatoes
- diced onions or scallions
- garlic, minced, pressed or garlic juice
- fresh, sliced mushrooms (may be sautéed first, if desired, to keep from drying out)
- dried gourmet mushrooms such as shitake
- broccoli florets, cooked until just tender, do not overcook
- cauliflower florets, cooked until just tender, do not overcook
- olives, pitted and sliced
- roasted red peppers, diced, found in jars

- jalapeño peppers, diced, sliced or pureed
- pimientos, diced
- chopped spinach, cooked first. Fresh is best on pizza but frozen is acceptable. If using frozen spinach, thaw, drain and pat dry with a paper towel. Sauté lightly in about a tablespoon of olive oil with or without garlic.
- asparagus
- carrots, diced or grated
- eggplant, cooked first (leftover eggplant Parmesan is great!)
- leeks
- capers
- bell peppers, any color. In fact using two or three different colors on a pizza gives a nice, colorful appearance and slightly different flavors.
- summer squash. Lightly sauté first in 1 tbs. olive oil with or without garlic. Drain on paper towels.
- mixed frozen vegetables. Use about $\frac{1}{2}$ lb., cooked until just tender.
- artichoke hearts

PROTEIN

Since pizza is usually a full meal unto itself, it is wise to use toppings which fulfill dietary needs. Pizza is not a junk food! Use lots of vegetables and protein and only enough cheese to flavor and you have a healthy meal! Remember that meats may be shredded or cut into attractive shapes rather than just *diced* or *sliced*, as I usually indicate in my recipes.

- cooked, crumbled bacon or diced or sliced Canadian bacon
- ground meat of any type, cooked, drained and crumbled
- sausage, cooked, drained and crumbled
- diced ham
- diced prosciutto. Ask the grocery deli to cut you a chunk instead of the thin slices they normally prepare of this salt-cured Italian ham.
- cooked, diced turkey or chicken (great use for leftovers). I use approximately $\frac{1}{2}$ cup cooked diced chicken or 1 boneless, skinless chicken breast. You may use more meat; however, I find that the center of the pizza does not cook as well if too many toppings are used.
- cooked, shredded beef
- cooked, peeled shrimp, chopped

- cooked scallops
- anchovies
- sliced or diced pepperoni
- sliced or diced salami

FRUITS

Yes, fruits may be used on traditional pizzas as well as nontraditional, sweet pizzas. Try pineapple chunks with pizza sauce and cheese with nothing else and you'll see what I mean.

- raisins
- pineapple chunks
- mandarin orange segments
- sliced apples

- sliced peaches
- sliced or diced strawberries
- seedless grapes - halved

NUTS AND SEEDS

Nuts and seeds add flavor and crunch to any pizza baking. Pine nuts (pignoli) are very common in Italian and Middle Eastern cooking, but also try sesame or sunflower seeds. Large seeds may tear the dough if rolling the dough for a very thin crust.

- pignoli (pine nuts)
- chopped walnuts
- chopped almonds

- sesame seeds
- sunflower seeds

In addition to the many toppings I have listed, use leftovers as pizza toppings. Leftover spaghetti sauce is a great substitute for pizza sauce. Eggplant or chicken Parmesan leftovers are wonderful pizza toppings. Even leftover corned beef could top a rye pizza. Leftover stir-fry is wonderful as is any leftover grilled meat. If you have meat which has been marinated in herbs or spices, use a complementary herbed or spiced dough to bring out the flavor. I quite often marinate and cook an extra chicken breast, dice it up and throw it in the freezer so I have ready-made cooked chicken when I want a quick pizza.

If you have a pizza party and ask people to bring a topping, you may want to give them a copy of these pages so they will start thinking about fun and festive toppings!

EQUIPMENT

UTENSILS AND PANS

As a general rule, the darker in color (usually a dark steel) the pan, the crispier the crust. If using pizza pans, the oven should be preheated for at least 30 minutes at 500°.

Thin Crust Pans - There are two types of thin crust pans available for sale, those with perforations and those without. The perforated pans give the pizza a nice, crispy crust and are preferable to the nonperforated pans. After the pizza is cooked, slide the pizza off the pan and cut it on a pizza tray or a cutting board so you won't damage the pan and cause the pizza to stick to the damaged section the next time you bake. The nonperforated pans are not to be confused with pizza serving trays, which are too thin to cook on. If you do not have a pizza pan, a cookie sheet could always be used in a pinch but will not have as crispy a crust. I have even baked a pizza in a cast-iron skillet (in the oven, not on the stovetop) and it turned out great but was small.

Pizza Serving Trays - These trays are very similar in appearance to a nonperforated pan but are used to slide the finished pizzas onto for cutting and serving. Buy one slightly larger than the size of pizza you make the most — it's easier to slice when you can grab a little of the pan to hold it still while cutting.

Deep Dish Pizza Pans - Deep dish pans are at least 1 to 2 inches deep. I use a deep dish, perforated pan which is $1\frac{1}{2}$ inches deep and 12 inches in diameter, and tends to crisp the bottom crust a little better. I also have a 2-inch-deep, 12-inch diameter pan which is a heavier, darker steel and tends to give the sides and bottom a hard crust. I'm sure there are some dark, perforated deep dish pans available but I have yet to find one!

Pan Removers - There are special "pan grabbers" which may be used to get the pans in and out of the oven instead of using oven mitts or pot holders.

Sicilian Pans - The traditional shape of a Sicilian pizza is square or rectangular. The pans are usually 1 inch deep. If using a 12-inch square pan, any of the deep dish doughs will work very well. A larger, rectangular shape pan may use the deep dish doughs for a slightly thinner crust. Sicilian pans are generally made out of a blue or black steel for a crusty crust and a light and tender interior. As with any pan, follow any special instructions for seasoning your particular pan.

Screens - Aluminum screens with a fairly heavy rim are made specifically for pizza baking. The screens should be brushed with olive oil or sprayed with a nonstick vegetable spray. Roll or hand stretch your pizza so that it is about the same size as your screen. Place your dough on the screen and crimp the sides of the dough to give your pizza a rim. Do not press the dough onto the screen as it could stick and be very difficult to remove. Spread your toppings on the pizza on the screen and then place your pizza, screen and all, either on a pizza stone or directly on your oven rack. Screens do not need to be washed after each use. Simply remove any food which has spilled onto it and brush it off. The screens may be washed occasionally.

Cooking Discs - These discs are a combination of a perforated pizza pan and a screen. They may be found in a black coating for a crispier crust and are somewhat heavier and more durable than screens. Coat the disc with oil or a nonstick spray every once in awhile to prevent the dough from sticking. Assemble your pizza on the disc and clean it the same way you would a screen.

Dockers - A docker is a rolling pin with tines embedded in it. It may be rolled over the dough, after the dough has been rolled or stretched into shape, so that it pierces the dough in order to prevent bubbling when baking without toppings. I find that using a fork or sharp knife every $\frac{1}{2}$ inch or so does the trick.

Peels - A long-handled wooden paddle, called a *peel*, is essential if baking pizza directly on a stone or tiles. Roll or hand stretch the dough so that it is just slightly smaller than your peel and your stone. Sprinkle the peel with a tablespoon (give or take) of cornmeal to prevent the dough from sticking and then place the dough on the peel. Crimp the sides to give your pizza a rim and then place your toppings on the pizza right on the peel. Once the pizza is assembled it is too difficult to place on the peel without dropping toppings all over the place! The pizza is then slipped off the peel directly onto the stone or tile.

It takes a little practice to use the peel, as you must place the peel on the stone and then quickly jerk your hand to remove the peel and leave the pizza centered on the stone. Pizzas with many toppings may tend to lose toppings during this procedure. If new to using a peel, I recommend practicing with pizzas with no extra toppings until you get the hang of it. Once you are comfortable, you may use some toppings, but do not overload the pizza as too many toppings may still slide off.

Stones and Tiles - Pizzas are traditionally baked in brick ovens at extremely high temperatures. To obtain results similar to pizzas baked in brick ovens, pizza stones or tiles may be used in home ovens, either gas or electric. The stones give an even heat distribution and absorb any moisture from the dough which results in a crispy, light crust. Place the stone directly on the bottom of a gas oven or on the lowest rack in an electric oven. The oven should be preheated to 500° for at least 1 hour prior to baking, which allows the stone to heat properly. The stone may be left in the oven at all times and used as a rack or just to help your oven maintain an even temperature and to absorb excess moisture.

The pizza may be slid onto the stone or tiles using a peel. If you feel uncomfortable using a pizza peel to slide a pizza onto or off of the stone, try using a pizza screen, cooking disc or a perforated pan directly on the stone — it will still crisp nicely. There are special wire racks available to carry the stone to the table for serving and warming the pizza. Just remember that these stones are extremely hot (and are generally heavy)!

Stones may discolor after use both from drippings and washings. This should not affect the baking results. Clean the stone occasionally with a scouring pad. If it has a lot of baked-on residue, clean it with an emery paper. Do not use soap on your stone as the soap may be absorbed and leave an aftertaste.

Pizza stones may also be used to bake bread, biscuits, tortillas or even cookies.

Cutting Wheels - Cutting wheels are a very helpful for homemade pizza. Look for at least a 2¼-inch wheel in a kitchen, gourmet or restaurant supply shop. Some pizza wheels even have replacement parts available.

PIZZA BAKERS

There are a few mini ovens which have been designed specifically for baking pizzas.

The **Pizza Express** imported by VillaWare is a mini pizza kiln with a pizza stone (see page 17). It comes with a pizza scoop (peel) which is cut in half so that you can assemble your pizza on the scoop, place it directly on the hot stone and remove both sides easily without losing toppings. The 12-inch stone cooks pizzas in 5 minutes. Call 800-822-1335 to locate stores near you which carry it.

The **Pizzadome** imported by Swissmar comes in two versions, an electric or a fondue burner version. Both versions have a clay "igloo" top with 3 or 4 openings for 4-inch (hors d'oeuvre size) individual pizzas. The entire oven may be placed in the center of a table so people can assemble and bake their own pizzas (on mini pizza spatulas). Call 800-387-5707 to locate stores near you which carry it.

The **Dazey Round-A-Bout** is a 14-inch diameter pizza oven, wok, griddle, fry pan and buffet server (great for pizza parties). The temperature ranges up to 425°, which is perfect for reheating pizza. Fresh pizza should be cooked longer at that temperature – precooked crusts work best. There are two lid sizes – look for the higher, dome lid to accommodate more toppings. Call 913-782-7500 for store locations.

GENERAL DOUGH MAKING TECHNIQUES

Whether you make the dough by hand or by a machine, get to know the way the dough feels and looks. It should always be a nice, round ball but not sticky to the touch. Adjust the dough if necessary by adding a tablespoon of water or flour at a time until it reaches the proper consistency. Flour absorbs moisture as it sits in the store or kitchen, so it would not be uncommon to require minor adjustments. The more moist the dough, the more tender the crust will be, so add flour sparingly — just enough to handle easily. All recipes in this book were tested using a bread machine or a yeast dough maker to knead the dough.

Bread Machine: Warm liquids to lukewarm, 110°. Add ingredients to your bread machine in the order specified for your machine. Use the dough cycle, which will knead the dough and allow it to rise one time. It is not necessary to let the dough rise any longer than 1 hour. If your machine has a double kneading dough cycle (DAK and Welbilt ABM 100), remove the dough after an hour or so and turn off your machine. Allowing the dough to knead the second time causes bubbles which are difficult to roll. Either active dry or rapid rise yeast may be used. It is not necessary to proof the yeast in water; just mix it in with the flour.

Dough Maker (yeast): Warm liquids to lukewarm, 110°. Place ingredients in your machine according to the directions for your machine. Either active dry or rapid rise yeast may be used. It is not necessary to proof the yeast in water; just mix it in with the flour. Remove dough from machine and place in a large greased bowl, cover with a kitchen towel and let rise in a warm, draft-free location for 50 to 60 minutes.

Food Processor: Warm liquids to lukewarm, 110°. Combine all dry ingredients (including yeast) in a food processor bowl (steel blade) and process for 10 seconds. Pour the oil and remaining liquid ingredients through the feeding tube until the dough forms a ball. If dough is sticky, add flour 1 tablespoon at a time until dough is not sticky. Process dough for about 1 minute or knead by hand for about 5 to 10 minutes. Shape dough into a ball, place in a greased bowl and cover with a kitchen towel. Place in a warm, draft-free location for 50 to 60 minutes. Either active dry or rapid rise yeast may be used. It is not necessary to proof the yeast in water; just mix it in with the flour.

Heavy-duty Mixer with Dough Hook: Prepare dough as you would for a dough maker or food processor. Allow to knead for about 5 minutes. Add just enough flour to cause the dough to cling to the dough hook. Allow dough to rise as in food processor instructions.

By Hand: If using a quick or rapid-rise yeast, mix it with the flour. There is no need to proof it. If using active dry yeast, place $\frac{1}{4}$ to $\frac{1}{3}$ of the warm water in a large bowl and sprinkle a pinch of sugar and the yeast into the water. Stir until dissolved and let sit in a warm, draft-free location for 5 minutes. Add remaining water (liquid) and oil and stir well. Add all remaining ingredients and stir together until you can no longer work the dough with a spoon. Turn out on a lightly floured counter. Pat the dough into a ball and flatten it slightly. Fold the dough over, and using the heels of your hands, push the dough away from you with a rolling motion. Rotate the dough one quarter each time you repeat this process. Continue kneading the dough for 5 to 10 minutes. Place the dough in a large greased bowl and cover it with a clean towel. Place it in a warm, draft-free location (such as an oven or microwave) and let rise for 50 to 60 minutes.

HINTS FOR SUCCESSFUL PIZZA BAKING

- Spray the pizza pan with nonstick vegetable spray or brush with olive oil. Dusting with cornmeal (or wheat germ) to prevent sticking is optional.

- Pizzas may be rolled out, topped and frozen or cooked, cooled and frozen. To heat, simply remove from freezer and bake without thawing first. It will take a little longer to cook.

- Make extra pizza dough, roll it out and place it on the pan, screen or peel. Brush it with olive oil (or melted garlic butter), and pierce the dough every $\frac{1}{2}$ inch or so with a fork (to prevent bubbles). Bake the shell in a preheated 500° oven for about 5 minutes. Allow to cool, stack with waxed paper in between, wrap well in plastic and freeze for up to 1 month. To use, remove dough from freezer (it is not necessary to thaw, but you may), brush dough with oil to prevent sogginess, top as desired and bake in a preheated 450° oven for 15 to 20 minutes. While it can be done, I do not recommend freezing the pizza dough itself.

- Pizza dough may be made and refrigerated, loosely wrapped in a plastic bag, for up to one week. Simply remove dough when needed, roll it out (it is easier to roll when cold!), top and bake. I always have pizza dough in the refrigerator for a quick pizza when I don't feel like cooking. Dough which has been refrigerated will result in a crispier crust. Use the dough within a week to a week and a half.

- If dough is difficult to roll or shape, place in a greased bowl, cover with a kitchen towel and place in the refrigerator for 5 to 10 minutes.

- Roll dough on a cornmeal-covered counter for an authentic pizza parlor taste. This also prevents the dough from absorbing too much flour. Roll or stretch the dough from the center outwards.

- For a crispy crust, roll the dough very thinly (about ¼ inch), top and bake immediately. For a softer, chewier crust, roll the dough to about ½ inch thickness and let rise for 10 to 30 minutes before topping and baking.

- Brush the dough with olive oil to prevent a soggy crust. This is optional and I find it useful only when using large amounts of cheeses and toppings.

- Arrange the toppings and cheese so the middle has less than the outer edges. This prevents the center from being undercooked as the ingredients tend to slide toward the middle during baking.

- Too much sauce and/or cheese will tend to pull the cheese and other topping ingredients towards the center. This results in undercooked dough which is difficult to hold and eat without falling apart. If this happens, use less sauce and/or cheese next time.

- One school of thought is to always lightly brush the dough with olive oil, spread the cheese next, the sauce on top of the cheese and then the toppings. I'm a creature of habit and always seem to put the tomato sauce directly on the dough. It is a matter of preference.

- For a softer, chewier crust, brush the edge of the crust with olive oil as soon as you remove the pizza from the oven. (I use a pastry brush) There are lots of olive oils on the market now which are flavored with garlic, pepper or even lemon which adds a nice flavor to your pizza.

- Allow pizza to cool for 2 to 3 minutes before slicing. This allows the cheese to set and it will slice easily and not slide off.

- Always slide the pizza off the screen, paddle or perforated pan and cut it on a pizza serving tray or cutting board. This prevents damage to your pan or screen. Use a good pizza wheel (2¼-inch is a good size) or kitchen shears to cut the pizza.

- Arrange the toppings creatively for the best eye appeal.

- The pizza dough may be shaped into small, individual pizzas or appetizer-size.

- To grill pizza: Use a medium-hot fire. Prebake pizza dough by brushing the dough lightly with olive oil and place it on the grill with or without a pan (I use a screen). It should cook in less than 1 minute. (Or prebake in your oven.) Once the shell has been prebaked, lower the temperature of the gas grill or allow the charcoal fire to subside slightly, top pizzas and cook. Watch carefully to avoid burning.

PIZZA PARTY IDEAS

Whether you are planning a birthday party for five-year-olds (maybe with a little extra adult help), a teen pizza party or an adult get-together, try hosting a pizza party. You may either supply all the ingredients or ask guests to bring one topping for pizza and you provide the sauce and dough. The dough could be rolled out and pre-baked (see page 23), or you may have your guests join in the fun of rolling out their own dough and selecting their toppings.

Another pizza get-together idea is a pizza bake-off. This could be with one friend or couple or with an entire neighborhood. When my husband was stationed at the U.S. Naval Postgraduate School in Monterey, California, we had a neighborhood get-together in the Navy Housing area. Every family was asked to bring a homemade pizza

— no frozen or pizza parlor pizzas allowed. The majority of families had never attempted to make a pizza before and everyone was scrambling around looking for recipes or directions — which was all part of the fun of it! We had a judging on crust and toppings, but most of all we had fun!

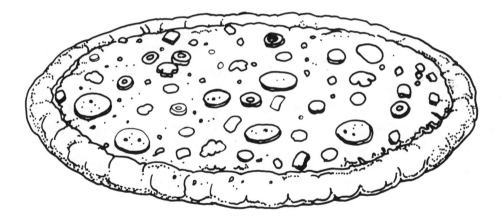

THIN CRUST PIZZA DOUGHS

GENERAL DIRECTIONS FOR THIN CRUST PIZZAS

1. Make thin crust dough according to *General Dough Making Techniques*, page 20.
2. Preheat your oven to 500° for at least 30 minutes if using a pan and at least 1 hour if using a stone.
3. Grease the pizza pan with olive oil or spray it with a nonstick vegetable spray. A light dusting of cornmeal to further prevent sticking is optional — it usually adds a little crunch and flavor to the dough. If using a peel and stone, dust the peel to prevent the dough from sticking so that you may easily slide it off the peel and onto the stone.
4. While the dough is rising, prepare your topping and grate your cheese; set aside. After the dough has risen 1 time, roll it out on a lightly floured or cornmeal-covered (I prefer cornmeal) countertop or hand stretch the dough into a circle. Pick up the dough and turn it over and roll or stretch from the center outwards until a circle is formed. It may never be a perfect circle but that adds to the uniqueness of your homemade pizza. Dust the dough only as needed to prevent sticking with either flour or cornmeal. The thinner you roll or stretch the dough, the thinner the crust. A thinly rolled dough which does not rise a second time (after rolling) will give you the thinnest, crispiest crust. Lay the dough on your

prepared pizza pan or peel. Pull the dough up around the edges of the pan so that a slight lip is formed, and crimp the edges.

5. For a thin, crispy crust, place your toppings on the pizza and bake immediately. For a thicker, chewier crust, allow the dough to rise for 15 to 30 minutes. The longer the rise, the thicker the dough. Place your toppings on after this second rising and then bake. The toppings should be placed in such a way that the rim is left unadorned (about ¼- to ½-inch border is good). This prevents spillage when baking and gives a nice piece of crust to hold when eating.

6. Place the pizza on the bottom rack of the oven or directly on the pizza stone and bake until the crust is golden brown and the cheese is melted. If the oven was properly preheated, it should only take 5 to 10 minutes to bake a thin crust pizza.

Precooked shells - Make extra pizza dough, roll it out and place it on the pan, screen or peel. Brush it with olive oil (or melted garlic butter), and pierce the dough every ½-inch or so with a fork (to prevent bubbles). Bake the shell in a preheated 500° oven for about 5 minutes. Allow to cool, stack with waxed paper in between, wrap it well in plastic and freeze for up to 1 month. To use, remove dough from freezer (it is not necessary to thaw but you may), brush dough with oil to prevent sogginess, top as desired and bake in a preheated 450° oven for 15 to 20 minutes.

Each recipe in this chapter makes approximately:

- one 15- or 16-inch thin crust pizza
- one 14-inch medium crust pizza
- two 10-inch medium crust pizzas
- three 10-inch thin crust pizzas
- four 8-inch thin crust pizzas
- three 8-inch medium crust pizzas
- four or five 6-inch individual pizzas
- four or five calzones

If you want a very thin crust and end up with excess dough, simply form it into bread sticks, brush with a little water and sprinkle some kosher salt, poppy seeds or sesame seeds on top. Bake them right beside your pizza.

BASIC THIN CRUST DOUGH

This is the result of many years of pizza dough testing. It is the perfect thin crust dough.

1 tsp. active dry yeast
2 cups bread flour
$\frac{1}{4}$ tsp. salt
1 tbs. olive oil
$\frac{2}{3}$ cup lukewarm water

Nutritional analysis per $\frac{1}{8}$ ***recipe*** *118 calories, 2.3 g fat, 3.9 g protein, 20.6 g carbohydrate, 0 mg cholesterol, 73.7 mg sodium*

SWEET THIN CRUST DOUGH

This is the perfect pizza dough for a dessert or breakfast pizza. Top with ricotta cheese and fruits such as sliced strawberries and blueberries for a real treat. This pizza should be rolled or stretched onto the pizza pan or screen, pricked with a fork every ½ inch and baked for 5 minutes in a preheated 350° oven. It may then be topped and baked in the 350° oven until done, about 5 to 10 minutes.

1 tsp. active dry yeast
2 cups bread flour
2 tbs. sugar
¼ tsp. salt
2 tbs. vegetable oil
1 egg
½ cup lukewarm milk

Nutritional analysis per ⅛ *recipe* *161 calories, 4.7 g fat, 5.2 g protein, 24.5 g carbohydrate, 26.9 mg cholesterol, 88.9 mg sodium*

POTATO THIN CRUST DOUGH I

Potato water is water in which potatoes have been boiled. The water makes this dough a soft, tender dough and adds nutrition as well. This is a basic dough which may be topped with anything.

1 tsp. active dry yeast
2 cups bread flour
½ tsp. sugar
¼ tsp. salt
1 tbs. olive oil
¾ cup lukewarm potato water

Nutritional analysis per ⅛ ***recipe*** *119 calories, 2.3 g fat, 3.9 g protein, 20.9 g carbohydrate, 0 mg cholesterol, 73.7 mg sodium*

POTATO THIN CRUST DOUGH II

A great way to get that potato flavor without boiling any potatoes! Top with anything.

1 tsp. active dry yeast
2 cups bread flour
¼ cup instant potato flakes
½ tsp. sugar
¼ tsp. salt
1 tbs. olive oil
⅔ cup lukewarm water

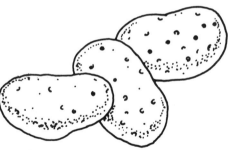

Nutritional analysis per ⅛ recipe   *126 calories, 2.3 g fat, 4.1 g protein, 22.4 g carbohydrate, 0 mg cholesterol, 75.6 mg sodium*

BUTTERMILK THIN CRUST DOUGH

A variation on a basic pizza dough crust. The buttermilk makes a soft, tender dough.

1 tsp. active dry yeast
2 cups bread flour
$\frac{1}{4}$ tsp. salt
$\frac{1}{2}$ tsp. baking soda
1 tbs. olive oil
$\frac{3}{4}$ cup lukewarm buttermilk

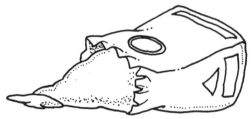

Nutritional analysis per $\frac{1}{8}$ recipe   127 calories, 2.5 g fat, 4.6 g protein, 21.7 g carbohydrate, 0.8 mg cholesterol, 149 mg sodium

PARMESAN THIN CRUST DOUGH

This is a lightly cheese-flavored variation of a basic dough which may be served with any type of topping. Make sure you use freshly grated cheese and not the stuff from the green can. Many grocery stores carry grated Parmesan in the refrigerated section which is a real time-saver.

1 tsp. active dry yeast
2 cups bread flour
$\frac{1}{4}$ tsp. salt
$\frac{1}{2}$ cup freshly grated Parmesan cheese
1 tbs. olive oil
$\frac{2}{3}$ cup lukewarm water

Nutritional analysis per $\frac{1}{8}$ recipe 141 calories, 3.8 g fat, 5.9 g protein, 20.8 g carbohydrate, 4 mg cholesterol, 167 mg sodium

THIN CRUST SOURDOUGH

Watch the dough carefully and adjust the amount of water or flour if necessary. Top with your favorite toppings.

1 tsp. active dry yeast
2 cups bread flour
$\frac{1}{4}$ tsp. salt
1 tbs. olive oil
1 cup sourdough starter
1-2 tbs. water, if and as necessary

Nutritional analysis per $\frac{1}{8}$ recipe *126 calories, 0.6 g fat, 4.6 g protein, 25.5 g carbohydrate, 0 mg cholesterol, 72.9 mg sodium*

SPINACH THIN CRUST DOUGH

Working with spinach can be tricky. It takes longer to knead the moisture out of the spinach. Keep an eye on the dough and adjust the consistency as necessary by adding a tablespoon of water or flour at a time until the dough forms a nice, round ball which is not too sticky. If you add too much water and the dough becomes stickier as it kneads, simply add flour until the proper consistency is obtained. Top with **Cheese Topping**, *page 122, or just about any topping you want.*

1 tsp. active dry yeast
2 cups bread flour
1/4 tsp. salt
1 clove of garlic, minced or pressed
1/2 to 1 tsp. lemon pepper, optional
1 tbs. olive oil
2/3 cup cooked, undrained chopped spinach
1-3 tbs. water, if and as necessary

Nutritional analysis per 1/8 recipe 122 calories, 2.3 g fat, 4.3 g protein, 21.3 g carbohydrate, 0 mg cholesterol, 83.9 mg sodium

NO RISE THIN CRUST DOUGH

This basic pizza dough is for those times you forgot to make the dough and don't have time for it to rise. It uses baking powder instead of the traditional yeast to leaven it. Watch it carefully as it takes a shorter time for the crust to cook.

1 tbs. baking powder
2 cups bread flour
$1/4$ tsp. salt
1 tbs. olive oil
$2/3$ - $3/4$ cup tap water

Mix together baking powder, flour and salt in a large bowl. Make a well in the center and add olive oil. Slowly add water as you stir dough, first by hand. Then knead the dough with your hands until it is soft but not sticky. Turn dough onto a floured surface and knead lightly for 1 to 2 minutes. Lightly pat dough onto greased pizza pans — do not stretch too thin. The pizza may be baked immediately.

Nutritional analysis per $1/8$ recipe 116 calories, 2.3 g fat, 3.5 g protein, 20.5 g carbohydrate, 0 mg cholesterol, 233 mg sodium

ORANGE POPPY SEED THIN CRUST DOUGH

This slightly sweet pizza dough needs little more than olive oil and cheese on top. If serving as a meal, cooked, diced chicken could be added also.

1 tsp. active dry yeast
2 cups bread flour
1/4 tsp. salt
1 1/2 tsp. poppy seeds
1/2 tsp. grated orange peel
1 tbs. olive or vegetable oil
1 tbs. honey
2/3 cup lukewarm orange juice

Nutritional analysis per 1/8 recipe *138 calories, 2.5 g fat, 4.1 g protein, 25 g carbohydrate, 0 mg cholesterol, 73.6 mg sodium*

PINEAPPLE THIN CRUST DOUGH

*Believe it or not, chunks of pineapple may be added to a plain pizza sauce and cheese pizza! This is also superb topped with **Hawaiian Topping**, page 127.*

1 tsp. active dry yeast
2 cups bread flour
¼ tsp. salt
1 tbs. olive oil
⅔ cup pineapple juice

Nutritional analysis per ⅛ *recipe* 130 calories, 2.3 g fat, 3.9 g protein, 23.5 g carbohydrate, 0 mg cholesterol, 73.4 mg sodium

LEMON PEPPER THIN CRUST DOUGH

Top this flavorful pizza dough with any seafood topping, **Spinach Topping**, *page 149, or* **Lamb Topping**, *page 136.*

1 tsp. active dry yeast
2 cups bread flour
$\frac{1}{4}$ tsp. salt
$\frac{1}{2}$ to 1 tsp. coarsely ground black pepper
1 tbs. olive oil
$\frac{1}{2}$ cup lukewarm water
2 tbs. lemon juice

Nutritional analysis per $\frac{1}{8}$ *recipe* 119 calories, 2.3 g fat, 3.9 g protein, 21 g carbohydrate, 0 mg cholesterol, 74.4 mg sodium

ORANGE GINGER THIN CRUST DOUGH

*This is superb topped with **Orange Chicken Topping**, page 128, or add the sugar and use as a base for **Fruit Topping**, page 137. The freshly grated ginger root may be replaced with ¼ tsp. of ground ginger.*

1 tsp. active dry yeast
2 cups bread flour
¼ tsp. salt
1 tsp. sugar, optional for a sweeter crust
1 tsp. freshly grated ginger root
1 tbs. sesame oil
⅔ cup lukewarm orange juice

__Nutritional analysis per__ ⅛ __recipe__   130 calories, 2.2 g fat, 4.0 g protein, 23.5 g carbohydrate, 0.0 mg cholesterol, 76.6 mg sodium

SCALLION THIN CRUST DOUGH

*Use both the white and green parts of the scallion (green onion) for this flavorful dough which may be topped with any seafood topping, any spicy sauce or **Chicken Feta Topping**, page 131.*

1 tsp. active dry yeast
2 cups bread flour
¼ tsp. salt
½ tsp. coarsely ground black pepper
3 green scallions (green onions), diced
2 tbs. olive oil
⅔ cup lukewarm water

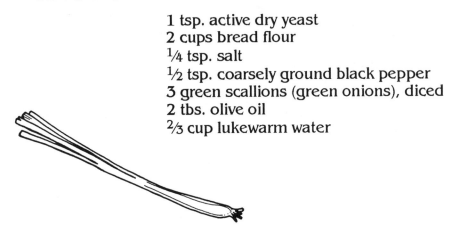

Nutritional analysis per ⅛ *recipe* *121 calories, 2.3 g fat, 4.1 g protein, 21.2 g carbohydrate, 0 mg cholesterol, 74.1 mg sodium*

BLACK BEAN THIN CRUST DOUGH

*A fabulous dough for any spicy or Mexican topping or **Brazilian Lemon Pepper Topping**, page 145.*

1 tsp. active dry yeast
2 cups bread flour
$\frac{1}{4}$ tsp. salt
$\frac{1}{2}$ cup lukewarm water
1 tbs. dried minced onion
$\frac{1}{2}$ tsp. cayenne pepper, optional
$\frac{1}{4}$ cup black bean puree

If using canned black beans, rinse and drain thoroughly and then process in a blender or food processor (steel blade) until pureed.

Nutritional analysis per $\frac{1}{8}$ recipe   113 calories, .6 g fat, 4.5 g protein, 22.4 g carbohydrate, 0 mg cholesterol, 98.1 mg sodium

JALAPEÑO THIN CRUST DOUGH

Top this basic dough with salsa and any of your favorite regular toppings like mushrooms or pepperoni. Boy, will people be surprised! Watch the dough and add water slowly until the dough obtains the proper consistency.

1 tsp. active dry yeast
2 cups bread flour
$1/4$ tsp. salt
2-3 tbs. chopped jalapeños with juice
1 tbs. olive oil
$1/2$ - $2/3$ cup lukewarm water

Nutritional analysis per $1/8$ ***recipe*** *125 calories, 2.4 g fat, 4.1 g protein, 22 g carbohydrate, 0 mg cholesterol, 152 mg sodium*

PARSLEY PEPPER THIN CRUST DOUGH

This great herbed pizza dough complements just about any topping you could think of. This is a good choice for a bring-your-own-topping pizza party (see page 26). If using chopped fresh parsley, use 3 tbs. or a scant ¼ cup.

1 tsp. active dry yeast
2 cups bread flour
¼ tsp. salt
1 tsp. coarsely ground black pepper
1 tbs. dried parsley
1 tbs. olive oil
⅔ cup lukewarm water

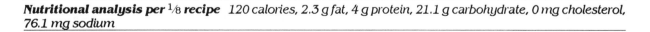

Nutritional analysis per ⅛ recipe   120 calories, 2.3 g fat, 4 g protein, 21.1 g carbohydrate, 0 mg cholesterol, 76.1 mg sodium

MINT THIN CRUST DOUGH

If you can find it, dried whole mint leaves really work wonders in this dough. They seem to have a much higher concentrated flavor than the dried, chopped mint found in grocery stores (which also works well!). If using chopped fresh mint, use 3 tbs. or a scant ¼ cup. This dough is superb topped with any Greek or Middle Eastern topping.

1 tsp. active dry yeast
2 cups bread flour
¼ tsp. salt
1 tbs. dried mint
1 clove garlic, minced or pressed
1 tbs. olive oil
⅔ cup lukewarm water

Nutritional analysis per ⅛ *recipe*   120 calories, 2.3 g fat, g protein, 21 g carbohydrate, 0 mg cholesterol, 74.7 mg sodium

THREE PEPPER THIN CRUST DOUGH

If you like pepper, this dough is for you! The crushed red pepper flakes may be replaced with ½ tsp. of cayenne if desired. This complements just about any topping you could think of.

1 tsp. active dry yeast
2 cups bread flour
¼ tsp. salt
1 tsp. coarsely ground black pepper
½ tsp. white pepper
1 tsp. crushed red pepper flakes
1 tbs. olive oil
⅔ cup lukewarm water

Nutritional analysis per ⅛ recipe 120 calories, 2.3 g fat, 3.9 g protein, 21.1 g carbohydrate, 0 mg cholesterol, 73.9 mg sodium

TOMATO BASIL THIN CRUST DOUGH

Any tomato based topping is good with this dough. A sure winner! Chopped fresh basil may be substituted for the dry — use 3 tbs. or a scant ¼ cup. One 5.5 oz. can of tomato juice equals ⅔ cup.

1 tsp. active dry yeast
2 cups bread flour
¼ tsp. salt
1 tbs. dried basil
1½ tbs. olive oil
⅔ cup lukewarm tomato juice

Nutritional analysis per ⅛ recipe   *130 calories, 3.2 g fat, 4.1 g protein, 21.8 g carbohydrate, 0 mg cholesterol, 114 mg sodium*

GARLIC HERB THIN CRUST DOUGH

A flavorful twist to a dough which complements a wide variety of toppings. If using fresh herbs, triple the amount given.

1 tsp. active dry yeast
2 cups bread flour
¼ tsp. salt
1 tsp. dried oregano
1 tsp. dried basil
2 cloves minced or pressed garlic
1 tbs. olive oil
⅔ cup lukewarm water

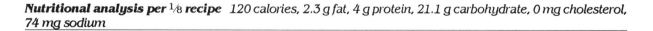

Nutritional analysis per ⅛ recipe   *120 calories, 2.3 g fat, 4 g protein, 21.1 g carbohydrate, 0 mg cholesterol, 74 mg sodium*

MEXICAN HERB THIN CRUST DOUGH

Contrary to the title, this is not just for Mexican toppings but will complement just about anything while adding just a little spice! if using chopped fresh cilantro, use 3 tablespoons or a scant ¼ cup.

1 tsp. active dry yeast
2 cups bread flour
1 tbs. dried cilantro
1 tsp. crushed red pepper flakes
1 tsp. oregano
¼ tsp. salt
1 tbs. olive oil
⅔ cup lukewarm water

Nutritional analysis per ⅛ *recipe* *119 calories, 2.3 g fat, 3.9 g protein, 20.9 g carbohydrate, 0 mg cholesterol, 73.8 mg sodium*

MEXICAN THIN CRUST DOUGH

Top this spicy dough with salsa and your choice of spicy toppings (see pages 142 to 145). I use a heaping teaspoon of diced jalapeños (packed in jars) when fresh jalapeños are not available. The fresh cilantro adds lots of flavor but if it is not available, substitute 1 tsp. dried.

1 tsp. active dry yeast
2 cups bread flour
1 tbs. fresh, chopped cilantro
¼ tsp. salt
½ tsp. crushed red pepper flakes
1 jalapeño pepper, diced, or equivalent
1 tbs. olive oil
1 clove minced or pressed garlic
⅔ cup lukewarm water

Nutritional analysis per ⅛ recipe *121 calories, 2.3 g fat, 4 g protein, 21.2 g carbohydrate, 0 mg cholesterol, 93.5 mg sodium*

CINNAMON THIN CRUST DOUGH

*Yes, cinnamon! The combination of cinnamon and tomatoes is very common in Mexican and Middle Eastern cooking. I think you'll find this to be a real winner! Serve with **Lebanese Topping**, page 136, or use the sugar and top with **Fruit Topping**, page 137.*

1 tsp. active dry yeast
2 cups bread flour
$\frac{1}{4}$ tsp. salt
1 tsp. ground cinnamon
1 tsp. sugar, optional, for a sweeter crust
1 tbs. olive oil
$\frac{2}{3}$ cup lukewarm water

Nutritional analysis per $\frac{1}{8}$ recipe 119 calories, 2.3 g fat, 3.9 g protein, 20.8 g carbohydrate, 0 mg cholesterol, 73.8 mg sodium

CILANTRO THIN CRUST DOUGH

Cilantro, the leaf of the coriander plant, has become very popular in the past couple of years and for good reason! Cilantro is often used in Mexican, Indian and Chinese cooking. It combines nicely with any tomato-based topping or (poultry) stir-fry topping. The flavor is really carried in the fresh cilantro and loses something when dried and ground. Only use dried (about 1 tbs.) if absolutely necessary. Fresh cilantro may be found in the produce section and dried in the spice section of some large grocery stores.

1 tsp. active dry yeast
2 cups bread flour
$\frac{1}{4}$ - $\frac{1}{3}$ cup chopped fresh cilantro
$\frac{1}{4}$ tsp. salt
$\frac{1}{2}$ tsp. coarsely ground black pepper, optional
1 tbs. olive oil
1 tbs. lime juice
$\frac{2}{3}$ cup lukewarm water

Nutritional analysis per $\frac{1}{8}$ recipe 119 calories, 2.3 g fat, 3.9 g protein, 20.8 g carbohydrate, 0 mg cholesterol, 73.7 mg sodium

---

GARLIC CHEESE THIN CRUST DOUGH

If prebaked, this is a wonderful substitute for the "Boboli" pizza shells found in your grocery store. Use either cheese or a combination of the two cheeses. This may be topped with anything and everything!

1 tsp. active dry yeast
2 cups bread flour
$\frac{1}{2}$ tsp. salt
$\frac{1}{4}$ tsp. sugar
$\frac{1}{2}$ cup grated mozzarella or provolone cheese
1 clove of garlic minced or pressed
1 tbs. olive oil
$\frac{2}{3}$ cup lukewarm water

Nutritional analysis per $\frac{1}{8}$ recipe 158 calories, 5.3 g fat, 6.6 g protein, 21 g carbohydrate, 11 mg cholesterol, 126 mg sodium

LEMON MINT THIN CRUST DOUGH

Toppings for this delicious dough may range from a simple tomato sauce and cheese with crushed red pepper flakes and mint to a **Chicken Feta Topping** *with mint, page 132.*

1 tsp. active dry yeast
2 cups bread flour
$\frac{1}{4}$ tsp. salt
1$\frac{1}{2}$ tsp. dried mint
$\frac{1}{2}$ tsp. lemon pepper
1 tbs. olive oil
$\frac{1}{2}$ cup lukewarm water
3 tbs. lemon juice

Nutritional analysis per $\frac{1}{8}$ ***recipe*** *120 calories, 2.3 g fat, 3.9 g protein, 21.2 g carbohydrate, 0 mg cholesterol, 75.2 mg sodium*

BASIC GARLIC THIN CRUST DOUGH

For garlic lovers everywhere! Top with anything. I keep a jar of minced garlic in the refrigerator for this dough, and use 2 heaping teaspoons.

1 tsp. active dry yeast
2 cups bread flour
$1/4$ tsp. salt
2-3 cloves garlic, minced or pressed
1 tbs. olive oil
$2/3$ cup lukewarm water

Nutritional analysis per $1/8$ ***recipe*** 119 calories, 2.3 g fat, 3.9 g protein, 20.9 g carbohydrate, 0 mg cholesterol, 74 mg sodium

JALAPEÑO CORN THIN CRUST DOUGH

Serve this tasty dough with any Southwestern or Mexican topping. Our favorite is salsa with black beans, diced onions, jalapeños and a combination of mozzarella and jack cheeses. Adjust the cornmeal as necessary to achieve the proper consistency.

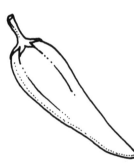

1 tsp. active dry yeast
1½ cups bread flour
½ - ⅔ cup cornmeal
¼ tsp. salt
1 tbs. olive oil
1-2 diced jalapeños
⅔ cup lukewarm water

Nutritional analysis per ⅛ recipe   135 calories, 2.7 g fat, 4.1 g protein, 24 g carbohydrate, 0 mg cholesterol, 255 mg sodium

ITALIAN HERB THIN CRUST DOUGH

The pepper adds a little "oomph" to this herb blend. This is a great dough for a "Bring Your Own Topping" pizza party. It goes with just about anything.

1 tsp. active dry yeast
2 cups bread flour
¼ tsp. salt
½ tsp. coarse black pepper
1 tsp. basil
1 tsp. oregano
½ tsp. thyme, optional
1 tbs. olive oil
⅔ cup lukewarm water

Nutritional analysis per ⅛ ***recipe*** *119 calories, 2.3 g fat, 3.9 g protein, 20.9 g carbohydrate, 0 mg cholesterol, 73.9 mg sodium*

FENNEL THIN CRUST DOUGH

*Serve up a great pizza with this dough and an Italian sausage or **Fennel Topping**, page 146. Variations of this dough may be made by using any seed such as anise, sesame, dill, celery or caraway.*

1 tsp. active dry yeast
2 cups bread flour
$\frac{1}{4}$ tsp. salt
1 tbs. fennel seed
$\frac{1}{4}$ tsp. coarsely ground black pepper
1 tbs. olive oil
$\frac{2}{3}$ cup lukewarm water

Nutritional analysis per $\frac{1}{8}$ **recipe**   *121 calories, 2.4 g fat, 4 g protein, 21.1 g carbohydrate, 0 mg cholesterol, 74.5 mg sodium*

ZAHTAR THIN CRUST DOUGH

Zahtar is a Middle Eastern spice blend which may be found in Middle Eastern shops or by mail order catalog. It is commonly used as a dip for pita bread and really flavors this dough. Add a little zahtar to your pizza sauce and throw on some pine nuts to pick up the flavor. Any other spice blend such as garam masala may be substituted.

1 tsp. active dry yeast
2 cups bread flour
1 tbs. zahtar spice blend
¼ tsp. salt
1 tbs. olive oil
⅔ cup lukewarm water

Nutritional analysis per ⅛ ***recipe*** *118 calories, 2.3 g fat, 3.9 g protein, 20.6 g carbohydrate, 0 mg cholesterol, 73.7 mg sodium*

GINGER THIN CRUST DOUGH

This is a superb pizza dough topped with any kind of Oriental stir-fry or with **Teriyaki Chicken Topping**, *page 130. The fresh ginger adds full-bodied flavor. Ground ginger may be substituted if desired — use ½ to 1 tsp.*

1 tsp. active dry yeast
2 cups bread flour
¼ tsp. salt
1 tsp. sugar
1 tbs. freshly chopped ginger root
1 tbs. vegetable oil
⅔ cup lukewarm water

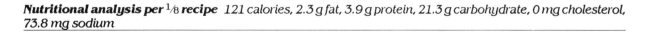

SPICY CORN THIN CRUST DOUGH

This is a great dough for a Mexican or spicy topping. Cayenne may be used in place of the crushed red pepper flakes — use ¼ tsp. Both the jalapeños and cayenne or crushed red pepper flakes may be omitted for a simple corn dough. Adjust the consistency of the dough with cornmeal or water if necessary.

1 tsp. active dry yeast
1½ cups bread flour
½ cup cornmeal
1 tsp. crushed red pepper flakes
1-2 jalapeños, diced
¼ tsp. salt
1 tbs. corn or vegetable oil
⅔ cup lukewarm water

Nutritional analysis per ⅛ recipe 146 calories, 2.5 g fat, 4.6 g protein, 26.3 g carbohydrate, 0 mg cholesterol, 97.6 mg sodium

AMARANTH THIN CRUST DOUGH

Amaranth grains are available at natural food stores or mail order catalogs. The grains themselves are very tiny and add a nutty flavor and texture to this winner of a pizza dough. Dating back to the Aztec Indians, amaranth is very high in calcium and low in calories. Quinoa, another ancient grain dating from the time of the Incas and recently growing in popularity, may be substituted for the amaranth.

1 tsp. active dry yeast
$\frac{1}{3}$ cup amaranth grains
2 cups bread or whole wheat flour
$\frac{1}{4}$ tsp. salt
1 tbs. olive oil
$\frac{3}{4}$ cup lukewarm water

Nutritional analysis per $\frac{1}{8}$ *recipe*   143 calories, 2.6 g fat, 4.9 g protein, 25 g carbohydrate, 0 mg cholesterol, 73.9 mg sodium

RYE THIN CRUST DOUGH

*Top this with ham and Swiss cheese for a favorite combination. For variety, substitute the caraway seeds with either anise or fennel seeds. If using fennel seeds, try topping with **Fennel Topping**, page 146.*

1 tsp. active dry yeast
1½ cups bread flour
½ cup rye flour
¼ tsp. salt
1 tbs. minced onion, optional
1 tsp. caraway seeds
1 tbs. olive or vegetable oil
⅔ cup lukewarm water

Nutritional analysis per ⅛ recipe 115 calories, 2.5 g fat, 3.8 g protein, 20.3 g carbohydrate, 0 mg cholesterol, 73.8 mg sodium

100% WHOLE WHEAT THIN CRUST DOUGH

The vital gluten enables the dough to be rolled easily. It may be purchased in some larger grocery stores or in natural food stores. If you elect not to use it, don't despair if the dough does not roll without tearing. Just keep at it and piece any tears together by hand.

2 tsp. active dry yeast
1 tbs. vital gluten
2 cups whole wheat flour
1/2 tsp. salt
1 tsp. sugar
2 tbs. olive oil
3/4 cup lukewarm water

Nutritional analysis per 1/8 **recipe** *120 calories, 2.3 g fat, 4.9 g protein, 22.1 g carbohydrate, 0 mg cholesterol, 147 mg sodium*

CRACKED WHEAT THIN CRUST DOUGH

Cracked wheat may be found in natural food stores or in some large grocery stores. This dough has a nice nutty taste and texture. For a whole grain dough, use whole wheat flour instead of the bread flour and add a teaspoon of vital gluten.

1½ tsp. active dry yeast
1½ - 1⅔ cups bread flour
½ cup cracked wheat
½ tsp. salt
1 tbs. olive oil
1 tbs. honey
⅔ cup lukewarm water

Nutritional analysis per ⅛ ***recipe*** *125 calories, 2.2 g fat, 3.9 g protein, 23.2 g carbohydrate, 0 mg cholesterol, 147 mg sodium*

SEVEN GRAIN THIN CRUST DOUGH

Any multi-grain cereal blend may be used in this dough. I use the 7, 9 or 12 grain blends which are found in natural food stores, mail order catalogs or even in some large grocery stores. This is a flavorful, crunchy dough.

1 tsp. active dry yeast
1¾ cups bread flour
½ cup multi-grain cereal
¼ tsp. salt
1 tbs. vegetable oil
1 tbs. honey
¾ cup lukewarm water

Nutritional analysis per ⅛ recipe 163 calories, 2.6 g fat, 5.4 g protein, 28.7 g carbohydrate, 0 mg cholesterol, 73.6 mg sodium

BRIOCHE THIN CRUST DOUGH

This dough makes a very rich crust which goes well with any topping. A small piece goes a very long way and will have guests asking for your recipe! The softness of the crumb is due to both the eggs and the all purpose (not bread) flour.

1 tsp. yeast
3 cups all purpose flour
2 tbs. sugar
$\frac{1}{2}$ tsp. salt
2 tbs. butter or margarine, melted
  and cooled to lukewarm
$\frac{1}{2}$ cup milk, lukewarm
2 large eggs

Allow dough to rise 1 time and then knead very briefly. Hand stretch and press onto a well greased thin crust pizza pan. Cover and let rise in a warm, draft-free location for 30 to 45 minutes. Top as usual and bake in a 350° oven (not the normal 500° oven) for 20 to 30 minutes or until crust is golden and cheese is melted.

Nutritional analysis per $\frac{1}{8}$ recipe   *220 calories, 4.5 g fat,, 6.8 g protein, 37.1 g carbohydrate, 53.5 mg cholesterol, 206 mg sodium*

DEEP DISH PIZZA DOUGHS

Doughs for deep dish pizzas are not just a higher proportion of ingredients than the thin crust pizzas. The largest difference is the high amount of oil and the use of sugar. Deep dish crusts have a tender interior. Deep dish pizzas and stuffed pizzas are usually eaten with a fork, unlike the thin crust pizzas.

GENERAL DIRECTIONS - DEEP DISH PIZZA

1. Make deep dish dough according to *General Dough Making Techniques*, page 20.
2. Preheat your oven to 475°.
3. Grease a 12-inch deep dish pan with olive oil or spray it with a nonstick vegetable spray.
4. After dough has risen one time, roll or hand stretch the dough into a circle so that it will completely cover the bottom of the pan. Pull the dough up around the edges of the pan so that a slight lip is formed.
5. Cover the pan with a kitchen towel and let the dough rise in a warm, draft-free location (microwave or on top of the oven) for approximately 30 minutes.
6. While the dough is rising, prepare your topping and grate your cheese; set aside.
7. Prick the dough several times with a fork (about every ½ inch) and bake the crust for 5 minutes.
8. Remove the crust from the oven, and using a pastry brush or your fingers, lightly cover the crust with olive oil.

9. Layer ingredients in this order: cheese, meats, sauce, vegetables and seasonings. Leave a $\frac{1}{2}$-inch border around the rim of the pizza.
10. Place pizza on bottom rack of oven and bake for 5 minutes, after which time, either move the pizza to the upper part of your oven or lower the temperature to 400°. Bake the pizza for 25 to 30 more minutes until the crust is golden brown.

Each deep dish dough recipe makes:
- one 12- to 14-inch deep dish, layered or stuffed pizza
- one 12-inch square Sicilian pizza (thinner crust if using a larger pan)
- two 15-inch thin crust pizzas
- three to four 6-inch individual deep dish pizzas

BASIC DEEP DISH DOUGH

You can't go wrong with a basic dough when having a bring-your-own-topping pizza party! Of course, you need some fun doughs too!

1½ tsp. active dry yeast
3 cups bread flour
½ tsp. salt
1 tsp. sugar
¼ cup olive oil
1 cup lukewarm water

__Nutritional analysis per__ ⅛ __recipe__   215 calories, 7.8 g fat, 31.3 g protein, 31.3 g carbohydrate, 0 mg cholesterol, 146 mg sodium

CHICAGO DEEP DISH DOUGH

Cornmeal is the secret ingredient in the dough which gives the Chicago pizza its special flavoring.

1½ tsp. active dry yeast
3 cups bread flour
⅓ cup cornmeal
½ tsp. salt
1 tsp. sugar
2 tbs. olive oil
1 cup lukewarm water

Nutritional analysis per ⅛ recipe   *233 calories, 7.9 g fat, 6.1 g protein, 35 g carbohydrate, 0 mg cholesterol, 162 mg sodium*

SOURDOUGH DEEP DISH DOUGH

Whether you are from San Francisco or Chicago, you'll love this one! Add the water only if and as needed. Starters vary with their liquid content.

$1\frac{1}{2}$ tsp. active dry yeast
3 cups bread flour
$\frac{1}{2}$ tsp. salt
1 tsp. sugar
2 tbs. olive oil
$\frac{3}{4}$ cup sourdough starter
$\frac{1}{2}$ cup lukewarm water

Nutritional analysis per $\frac{1}{8}$ recipe 220 calories, 4.4 g fat, 6.5 g protein, 38.8 g carbohydrate, 0 mg cholesterol, 146 mg sodium

CHEESE DEEP DISH DOUGH

This is a richer dough than the basic deep dish which complements any and all toppings.

1½ tsp. active dry yeast
3 cups bread flour
½ tsp. salt
1 tsp. sugar
½ cup freshly grated Parmesan or mozzarella cheese
3 tbs. olive oil
1 cup lukewarm milk

Nutritional analysis per ⅛ recipe   228 calories, 7.6 g fat, 8 g protein, 32.4 g carbohydrate, 6 mg cholesterol, 180 mg sodium

SPINACH DEEP DISH DOUGH

A wonderful deep dish or stuffed pizza dough. Add water only after the dough has been kneaded for at least 5 to 10 minutes, which allows the kneading to pull the moisture from the spinach. If you add water too soon (or too much), you may end up with a soggy dough. Don't despair, simply add a little flour until the correct consistency is obtained.

$1\frac{1}{2}$ tsp. active dry yeast
3 cups bread flour
$\frac{1}{2}$ tsp. salt
1 tbs. sugar
3 tbs. olive oil
1 pkg. (10 oz.) frozen chopped spinach, thawed, undrained and uncooked
1-2 tbs. lukewarm water, if and as needed

Nutritional analysis per $\frac{1}{8}$ recipe 213 calories, 6.1 g fat, 6.6 g protein, 33.7 g carbohydrate, 0 mg cholesterol, 163 mg sodium

WHOLE WHEAT DEEP DISH DOUGH

A healthier version of a deep dish dough. Sesame or crushed sunflower kernels could be added for a little crunch and flavor.

1½ tsp. active dry yeast
1½ cups bread flour
1½ cups whole wheat flour
½ tsp. salt
1 tsp. sugar
¼ cup olive oil
1 cup lukewarm water

Nutritional analysis per* ⅛ *recipe *215 calories, 7.8 g fat, 6.0 g protein, 32 g carbohydrate, 0 mg cholesterol, 147 mg sodium*

WHOLE GRAIN WHEAT DEEP DISH DOUGH

You will like this wonderful whole grain crust. A multi grain flour or cereal blend (4, 7, 9 or 12 grain) may be substituted for the cracked wheat.

1½ tsp. active dry yeast
2½ cups whole wheat flour
½ cup cracked wheat
½ tsp. salt
1 tsp. vital gluten, optional
2 tbs. olive oil
1 tbs. honey
1 cup lukewarm water

Nutritional analysis per ⅛ ***recipe*** *198 calories, 4.2 g fat, 6.3 g protein, 36.7 g carbohydrate, 0 mg cholesterol, 149 mg sodium*

SPICY CORN DEEP DISH DOUGH

This makes a wonderful, spicy focaccia with sliced jalapeños, minced garlic and/or diced onions pushed into the dough and cilantro, basil or oregano as the herb topping. It also complements any Mexican or spicy topping or filling.

1½ tsp. active dry yeast
3 cups bread flour
⅓ cup cornmeal
½ tsp. salt
1½ tsp. crushed red pepper flakes
1 tsp. coarsely ground black pepper
1 tsp. sugar
¼ cup olive oil
1 cup lukewarm water

Nutritional analysis per ⅛ recipe 239 calories, 7.9 g fat, 6.1 g protein, 35.3 g carbohydrate, 0 mg cholesterol, 162 mg sodium

CARAWAY PEPPER DEEP DISH DOUGH

*This will receive rave reviews as a stuffed pizza with **Broccoli and Cheese Stuffing**, page 111, or as a deep dish with a broccoli topping, page 150. Anise or fennel may be substituted for the caraway.*

$1\frac{1}{2}$ tsp. active dry yeast
3 cups bread flour
$\frac{1}{2}$ tsp. salt
1 tbs. caraway seed
1 tsp. coarsely ground black pepper
$\frac{1}{4}$ cup olive oil
2 tbs. honey
$\frac{3}{4}$ cup lukewarm water

Nutritional analysis per $\frac{1}{8}$ ***recipe*** *231 calories, 7.8 g fat, 5.7 g protein, 35.4 g carbohydrate, 0 mg cholesterol, 146 mg sodium*

GARLIC HERB DEEP DISH DOUGH

This fabulous dough stands on its own as a focaccia or for a deep dish with any tomato-based sauce or topping. Any of your favorite herbs such as cilantro, oregano, rosemary or mint may be substituted for the basil. This makes a fabulous thick focaccia with garlic or onion and the same or complementary herb on top.

1½ tsp. active dry yeast
3 cups bread flour
½ tsp. salt
1 tsp. sugar
2 tsp. dried basil or 2 tbs. fresh
2 cloves garlic, minced or pressed
¼ cup olive oil
1 cup lukewarm water

Nutritional analysis per ⅛ *recipe*   *216 calories, 7.8 g fat, 5.7 g protein, 31.6 g carbohydrate, 0.0 mg cholesterol, 146 mg sodium*

LEMON PEPPER DEEP DISH DOUGH

Use this with any Greek or Oriental topping or filling or as a focaccia with garlic and mint.

1½ tsp. active dry yeast
3 cups bread flour
½ tsp. salt
1-1½ tsp. coarsely ground black pepper
1 tsp. dried or 1 tbs. fresh mint, optional for a
    mint-flavored dough
1 tsp. sugar
¼ cup olive oil
2 tbs. lemon juice
¾ cup lukewarm water

Nutritional analysis per ⅛ recipe 216 calories, 7.8 g fat, 5.7 g protein, 31.7 g carbohydrate, 0 mg cholesterol, 147 mg sodium

TOMATO BASIL DEEP DISH DOUGH

A wonderful dough which may be used with just about any topping or filling. It makes a wonderful, festive-looking focaccia with olive oil, fresh basil and coarse salt.

1½ tsp. active dry yeast
3 cups bread flour
½ tsp. salt
1½ tsp. dried basil, or 1½ tbs. fresh
1 tsp. sugar
¼ cup olive oil
1 cup tomato juice

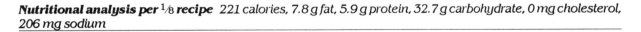

Nutritional analysis per ⅛ *recipe* 221 calories, 7.8 g fat, 5.9 g protein, 32.7 g carbohydrate, 0 mg cholesterol, 206 mg sodium

MEXICAN HERB DEEP DISH DOUGH

This makes a fabulous focaccia with garlic and cilantro or accompanies any spicy Mexican or Oriental topping or filling. Top with some frozen "stir-fry" vegetables which have been slightly sautéed or steamed for a healthy, tasty pizza.

$1\frac{1}{2}$ tsp. active dry yeast
3 cups bread flour
$\frac{1}{4}$ cup cornmeal
$\frac{1}{2}$ tsp. salt
$1\frac{1}{2}$ tsp. dried cilantro or $1\frac{1}{2}$ tbs. fresh
1 tsp. sugar
1 tbs. lime juice
2 cloves minced or pressed garlic
$\frac{1}{4}$ cup olive oil
1 cup lukewarm water

Nutritional analysis per $\frac{1}{8}$ recipe 216 calories, 7.8 g fat, 5.7 g protein, 31.5 g carbohydrate, 0 mg cholesterol, 146 mg sodium

PARSLEY PEPPER DEEP DISH DOUGH

A terrific accompaniment to just about any filling or topping. It stands alone as a focaccia with garlic and parsley and/or mint.

1½ tsp. active dry yeast
3 cups bread flour
¼ cup fresh parsley or 1½ tbs. dried
½ tsp. salt
1½ tsp. coarsely ground black pepper
1 tsp. sugar
¼ cup olive oil
¾ cup lukewarm water

Nutritional analysis per ⅛ recipe 217 calories, 7.8 g fat, 6.0 g protein, 32.6 g carbohydrate, 0 mg cholesterol, 148 mg sodium

THREE PEPPER DEEP DISH DOUGH

A very spicy dough! Serve with any of your favorite toppings or fillings. It is great with nothing more than olive oil lightly brushed on top and a little coarse salt to taste — bake as a focaccia.

1½ tsp. active dry yeast
3 cups bread flour
½ tsp. salt
2 tsp. coarsely ground black pepper
2 tsp. crushed red pepper flakes or 1 tsp. cayenne
1 tsp. white pepper
1 tsp. sugar
¼ cup olive oil
1 cup lukewarm water

Nutritional analysis per ⅛ *recipe* *218 calories, 7.8 g fat, 5.8 g protein, 32.2 g carbohydrate, 0 mg cholesterol, 146 mg sodium*

FLAKY DEEP DISH DOUGH

*This is similar to a croissant dough, flaky and delicious. While any topping may be used, I prefer a sweet one such as **Brie with Almond Topping**, page 140.*

1 tsp. yeast
2 cups bread flour
2 tbs. sugar

1 tsp. salt
²⁄₃ cup lukewarm milk
¹⁄₂ cup butter or margarine, softened

Knead dough in a machine or by hand until a satiny, smooth ball is obtained. Place dough in a greased bowl or plastic bag (not tightened) in the refrigerator for 6 to 8 hours to rise slowly. Roll dough into a large circle and spread butter over top. Fold dough up from the edges in about 5 places so butter is entirely encased and dough is easily shaped into a circle for rolling again. Place dough in a greased bowl or plastic bag and refrigerate for 30 minutes to prevent dough from warming and allowing butter to break through dough. Roll dough into a 12-inch circle and place in a greased 12-inch deep dish pizza pan. Cover and let rise in a warm, draft-free location for 30 to 40 minutes. Top with your favorite topping and bake in a preheated 350° oven for 20 to 30 minutes or until golden brown.

Nutritional analysis per ¹⁄₈ recipe *228 calories, 11.9 g fat, 4.4 g protein, 24.4 g carbohydrate, 0.3 mg cholesterol, 449 mg sodium*

STUFFED PIZZAS, CALZONES AND FOCACCIAS

GENERAL DIRECTIONS FOR CALZONES

Calzones are meat- and/or cheese-filled turnovers. They may be eaten either hot or cold.

1. Make thin crust dough according to *General Dough Making Techniques*, page 20.
2. Roll or stretch the dough into four or five 6-inch circles.
3. Place 2 to 4 tablespoons of filling on half of the circle, leaving a ¼- to ½-inch rim around the side. Do not overfill or it will be difficult to seal and the filling will seep out of the seam.
4. Dip a pastry brush in water or egg white and lightly moisten the edges of the dough.
5. Fold the dough over the side with the filling so that the filling is encased and seal the edges tightly by pressing shut with fingers or pressing together with a fork.
6. Brush each calzone lightly with olive oil, a beaten egg or cold water.
7. Bake in a preheated 500°oven for 20 to 25 minutes.

GENERAL DIRECTIONS FOR STROMBOLI

A stromboli roll is a stuffed, rolled pizza which may be eaten either hot or cold. It is a perfect treat for a picnic, tail gate party or boating. Cook ahead of time and serve by cutting into slices. Use either a topping or a filling as a stuffing. While a similar pizza roll may be made by simply jelly rolling, I find that the three-way fold of strombolis holds the filling better both when cooking and eating.

1. Prepare any thin crust dough according to *General Dough Making Techniques*, page 20.
2. After the first rising, roll dough into a rectangle.
3. Spread filling ingredients over the middle third of the rectangle so it runs the length of the wide end.
4. Fold one side over the top of the filling and then the other side on top of that. Pinch ends closed.
5. Place seam side down on a lightly greased pizza sheet or baking sheet.
6. Pierce top with a sharp knife or fork in 3 or 4 places and brush top lightly with olive oil.
7. Bake in a preheated 400° oven for 30 to 45 minutes or until done.

GENERAL DIRECTIONS FOR STUFFED PIZZA

Stuffed pizza is a two-layer pizza with meat and/or cheese sandwiched between layers of dough. A stuffed pizza may have either a pizza sauce or just a little olive oil on top. It is made in a deep dish pan and eaten with a fork. Any deep dish dough may be used.

1. Make deep dish dough according to *General Dough Making Techniques*, page 20.
2. While the dough is rising, prepare the filling and sauce.
3. Preheat your oven to 450°.
4. Grease a 12-inch deep dish pan with olive oil or spray it with a nonstick vegetable spray.
5. Divide the dough into two parts: one part should be approximately ⅔ of the total and the remaining ⅓ should be placed in an oiled bowl, covered with a kitchen towel and placed in a warm, draft-free location.
6. Roll or hand stretch the large section of dough into a circle so that it is about 13 to 14 inches in diameter. Lay the dough in the deep dish pan so that the dough completely covers the bottom of the pan and the excess dough comes up the sides and hangs slightly over the edge.

7. Place the filling on top of dough so that it evenly fills the bottom of the pan.
8. Roll remaining ⅓ of dough into a 12-inch circle and place on top of the filling. Fold the bottom edge of the dough over the top piece and crimp the two together so that they form a rim around the sides of the pizza.
9. Using a sharp knife or fork, pierce the top in 2 or 3 places to allow steam to escape.
10. Lightly brush top with 1 to 2 tbs. of olive oil or about ¼ cup of pizza sauce and a tablespoon or two of freshly grated Parmesan cheese.
11. Cover the pan with a kitchen towel and let the dough rise in a warm, draft-free location for 10 to 15 minutes.
12. Place pizza on bottom rack of oven and bake for 10 minutes, after which time either move the pizza to the upper part of your oven or lower the temperature to 400°. Bake the pizza for 30 to 40 more minutes until the crust is golden brown.

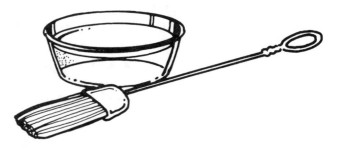

GENERAL DIRECTIONS FOR LAYERED PIZZA

A layered pizza is a variation of a stuffed pizza with the stuffing ingredients layered similar to lasagna. the sauce is layered inside so it is not used as a topping.

1. Make deep dish dough according to *General Dough Making Techniques*, page 20.
2. While the dough is rising, prepare the filling and sauce (³⁄₄ to 1 cup sauce).
3. Preheat your oven to 450°.
4. Grease a 12-inch deep dish pan with olive oil or spray it with a nonstick vegetable spray.
5. Divide the dough into two parts: one part should be approximately ²⁄₃ of the total and the remaining ¹⁄₃ should be placed in an oiled bowl, covered with a kitchen towel and placed in a warm, draft-free location.
6. Roll or hand stretch the large section of dough into a circle so that it is about 13 to 14 inches in diameter. Lay the dough in the deep dish pan so that the dough completely covers the bottom of the pan and the excess dough comes up the sides and hangs slightly over the edge.
7. Spread enough sauce on bottom of dough to cover it.
8. Place approximately ¹⁄₃ of the filling on top of dough so that it evenly fills the

bottom of the pan.

9. Add any extra cheese if desired.
10. Repeat the layers, sauce, filling, and cheese until pizza is almost to the top of the pan.
11. Roll remaining $\frac{1}{3}$ of dough into a 12-inch circle and place on top of the filling. Fold the bottom edge of the dough over the top piece and crimp the two together so that they form a rim around the sides of the pizza.
12. Using a sharp knife or fork, pierce the top in 2 or 3 places to allow steam to escape.
13. Lightly brush top with 1 to 2 tbs. of olive oil or a beaten egg.
14. Cover the pan with a kitchen towel and let the dough rise in a warm, draft-free location (microwave or on top of the oven) for 10 to 15 minutes.
15. Bake the pizza in the preheated 450° oven for 30 to 40 minutes until the crust is golden brown.

GENERAL DIRECTIONS FOR FOCACCIA

Focaccia (foh-CAH-chee-ah) breads may be made out of any pizza dough. I prefer the deep dish doughs made in a 12-inch, greased deep dish as the bread is thicker and has a tender interior. Any thin crust pizza dough may be used to make a thinner, crispier focaccia. Focaccia may be served hot or cold as a side bread with any meal or as an appetizer. Thick focaccias may be cut in half and filled for sandwiches.

1. Make deep dish or thin crust dough of choice according to *General Dough Making Techniques*, page 20.
2. Preheat your oven to 400°.
3. Grease a 12-inch deep dish pizza or cake pan with olive oil or spray it with a nonstick vegetable spray. If you don't have a deep dish pan, a cookie pan will do — just pat the dough into a 12-inch square or circle.
4. After dough has risen one time, hand stretch the dough into a circle so that it will completely cover the bottom of the pan.
5. Cover the pan with a kitchen towel and let the dough rise in a warm, draft-free location for approximately 30 minutes.
6. Prepare your topping and set aside.
7. After dough has risen, press fingertips into the dough to form small indentations.

8. If using garlic, onion, peppers or other similar vegetables, press small pieces into the indentations. Pour olive oil with herb(s) over top and sprinkle with coarse salt.
9. Place focaccia on bottom rack of oven or on a baking stone and bake for 25 to 30 minutes for a deep dish focaccia or 20 minutes for a thin crust focaccia.

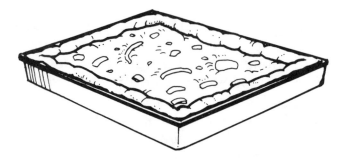

BASIC FOCACCIA

Focaccia is traditionally topped with slivers of garlic, basil or rosemary and a coarse salt. Following the recipe I have listed several different doughs and suggested herbs to accompany it. Feel free to adjust the amount of herbs to your taste. Use any one or a combination of herbs suggested. Let these suggestions serve as a springboard for your own imagination — focaccias are truly unlimited! If watching your weight, use the lesser amount of olive oil. For different flavors, try using walnut, macadamia or sesame oils instead of the olive oil.

2-3 cloves garlic, finely slivered or $\frac{1}{4}$
  cup finely slivered red onion
2 tbs. - $\frac{1}{4}$ cup olive oil

1 tbs. freshly chopped herbs or 1 tsp.
  dried herbs
coarse salt (Kosher or sea) to taste

After dough has risen one time, press it into a greased 12-inch pan. Cover with a kitchen towel and let rise in a warm, draft-free location for about 30 minutes. Press the slivers of garlic into the dough. Lightly brush olive oil over dough. Cover dough with herbs and salt. Bake on the bottom rack or on a stone in a preheated 400° oven for 30 to 35 minutes for a deep dish focaccia or 20 minutes for a thin crust focaccia.

Nutritional analysis per $\frac{1}{8}$ recipe without dough   *47 calories, 5.3 g fat, 0.1 g protein, 0.5 g carbohydrate, 0 mg cholesterol, 72.3 mg sodium*

SUGGESTED FOCACCIA COMBINATIONS

DOUGH	PAGE	GARLIC/SUBSTITUTE	HERB
Tomato Basil	52 or 87	garlic or onion	basil
Orange Ginger	45	fresh ginger root slivers	cilantro or mint
Spicy Corn	66 or 83	diced jalapeños	crushed red pepper flakes
Lemon Pepper	44 or 86	garlic or onion	mint, basil or oregano
Garlic Herb	53 or 85	garlic or onion	basil, oregano or
Mexican (Basic)	55	garlic, onion, jalapeños	cilantro
Cilantro	57	garlic, onion, jalapeños	cilantro
Spinach	40 or 80	garlic or onion	marjoram, mint, rosemary, tarragon, basil
Parsley Pepper	49 or 89	garlic or onion	parsley, basil, oregano
Mint	50	garlic or onion	mint
Three Pepper	51 or 90	garlic or onion	basil, mint, or cilantro
Mexican Herb	54 or 88	pimientos, jalapeños	cilantro
Basic Garlic	60	garlic or onion	anything goes!
Italian Herb	62	garlic or onion	basil, oregano, thyme, rosemary, tarragon
Scallion	46	garlic or onion	anything goes!
Zahtar	64	garlic or onion	zahtar
Fennel	63	garlic or onion	fennel seeds

WALNUT FOCACCIA

*Use **Basic Pizza Dough,** page 33, **Basic Deep Dish Dough**, page 76, or **Cheese Deep Dish Dough**, page 79, which will enable the flavor of the nuts to come through.*

2 tbs. - $\frac{1}{4}$ cup walnut oil, separated
$\frac{1}{4}$ cup walnuts
$\frac{1}{4}$ cup freshly grated Parmesan cheese

After dough has risen one time, press it into a greased 12-inch pan. Cover with a kitchen towel and let rise in a warm, draft-free location for about 30 minutes. While it is rising, heat 1 tablespoon of walnut oil in a medium skillet. Toast walnuts over low heat for 2 to 3 minutes, stirring constantly. Set aside. Lightly brush remaining walnut oil over dough. Press walnuts into the dough and sprinkle cheese on top. Bake on the bottom rack or on a stone in a preheated 400° oven for 30 to 35 minutes for a deep dish focaccia or 20 minutes for a thin crust focaccia.

Nutritional analysis per $\frac{1}{8}$ recipe without dough 66 calories, 6.5 g fat, 2 g protein, 0.6 g carbohydrate, 2 mg cholesterol, 46.6 mg sodium

DESSERT FOCACCIA

*Use **Sweet Pizza Dough**, page 34, or **Cinnamon Pizza Dough**, page 56, for this crispy, sweet treat. Serve as a dessert "cookie" with ice cream or as a breakfast treat.*

2 tbs. melted butter or margarine
2 tbs. sugar
1 tsp. cinnamon

After dough has risen one time, press it onto a greased 15-inch pizza pan or a baking sheet. Cover with a kitchen towel and let rise in a warm, draft-free location for about 15 minutes. Lightly brush melted butter over dough. Mix together sugar and cinnamon and sprinkle on top of crust. Bake on the bottom rack or on a stone in a preheated 400° oven for 20 minutes.

Nutritional analysis per 1/8 recipe without dough 38 calories, 2.9 g fat, 0 g protein, 3.2 g carbohydrate, 0 mg cholesterol, 37.6 mg sodium

RAISIN FOCACCIA

*Use **Orange Poppy Seed Dough**, page 42, or **Cinnamon Dough**, page 56 for this delicious alternative to raisin toast.*

3 tbs. melted butter or margarine
1 tsp. cinnamon
3-4 tbs. raisins

After dough has risen one time, press it into a greased 12-inch deep dish pizza or cake pan. Cover with a kitchen towel and let rise in a warm, draft-free location for about 30 minutes. Press raisins into dough. Mix cinnamon into melted butter or margarine and lightly brush over dough. Bake on the bottom rack or on a stone in a preheated 400° oven for 20 minutes.

Nutritional analysis per 1/8 recipe without dough 52 calories, 4.3 g fat, 0.2 g protein, 3.8 g carbohydrate, 0 mg cholesterol, 56.9 mg sodium

BASIC CHEESE FILLING FOR STUFFED PIZZA, LAYERED PIZZA OR CALZONES

Add your favorite herb to complement the dough being used. Diced meats such as ham, cooked sausage or ground meats may be added as well. Add cooked (steamed or sautéed), diced vegetables such as broccoli, mushrooms, spinach, etc., for extra flavor and nutrition. Remember that adding ingredients increases the amount of the filling. Any leftover filling may be refrigerated for a few days or frozen for several weeks for later use. Makes approximately 2½ cups for one stuffed or layered 15-inch pizza or 8 to 10 calzones (two dough recipes).

1 egg, beaten
1 container (15 oz.) ricotta cheese
1 green onion (scallion), diced with
  green part, optional
½ cup freshly grated Parmesan cheese

salt and pepper to taste
1 tsp. dried herbs or 1 tbs. chopped
  fresh herbs
1-2 cups grated or shredded
  mozzarella cheese

Mix ingredients together until well blended.

Nutritional analysis per ⅛ recipe without dough 180 calories, 12.0 g fat, 13.3 g protein, 2.7 g carbohydrate, 67.7 mg cholesterol, 545 mg sodium

CREAMY CILANTRO FILLING

*This is really a cross between a pesto and all-cheese topping which complements either **Basic Garlic Dough**, page 60, or **Three Pepper Dough**, page 51 or 90.*

1 cup fresh cilantro leaves, tightly packed
2-3 cloves garlic
¼ cup chopped red onion
1-2 jalapeños, diced
1 cup ricotta cheese
1 cup grated mozzarella cheese

Process cilantro, garlic, onion, and jalapeños in a food processor or blender until finely chopped and blended. Place mixture in a large bowl and mix in cheeses until well blended. Use as a filling for stuffed pizza or calzones.

Nutritional analysis per ⅛ recipe without dough   98 calories, 7.1 g fat, 6.4 g protein, 2.3 g carbohydrate, 26.7 mg cholesterol, 98.9 mg sodium

CREAMY BASIL FILLING

Mint could also be used for this flavorful filling. About ¼ cup of pine nuts could be added to this for a little crunch and flavor.

½ cup basil leaves, tightly packed
1-2 cloves garlic, minced or pressed
½ tsp. coarsely ground black pepper
½ cup or 2 oz. feta cheese, crumbled
2 cups grated mozzarella cheese

Process basil leaves, garlic and pepper in a blender or food processor (steel blade) until herbs are chopped and finely blended; remove to large bowl. Add cheeses, mixing well. Use as filling for stuffed pizza or calzones. If using this filling for stuffed pizza, cover the top with a pizza sauce.

Nutritional analysis per ⅛ recipe without dough   *114 calories, 8.6 g fat, 7.4 g protein, 2.1 g carbohydrate, 33.0 mg cholesterol, 157 mg sodium*

SAUSAGE FILLING

This is great as a filling for calzones or a stuffed pizza (with pizza sauce on top). Use either mild or hot Italian sausage. I cook the sausage in bulk and freeze in smaller portions for a quick microwave defrost and easy pizza. Cooked, chopped broccoli could be added if desired.

1 tbs. olive oil
¼ medium onion, diced
1-2 cloves garlic, minced
1 lb. Italian sausage
1 cup grated mozzarella cheese
1 cup grated provolone cheese
salt and pepper to taste

In a medium skillet, heat oil. Cook onion, garlic and sausage until sausage is browned and onion and garlic are softened. Drain well, add cheese and season to taste.

Nutritional analysis per ⅛ recipe without dough *299 calories, 23.1 g fat, 18.6 g protein, 3.6 g carbohydrate, 63.5 mg cholesterol, 830 mg sodium*

GREEK PESTO FILLING

*Use **Lemon Pepper Dough**, page 44, for this unbelievably delicious stuffed pizza or calzones.*

1 cup fresh mint leaves, tightly packed
2-3 cloves garlic
1/4 cup pine nuts or walnuts
salt and pepper to taste
1/4 cup olive oil
1/4 cup freshly grated Parmesan cheese
1/4-1/2 lb. cooked shrimp, diced, or 1/2
  cup cooked chicken, diced

2 cups grated mozzarella cheese
2-3 oz. or 1/2 cup crumbled feta cheese
black olives, pitted and halved, optional
2 to 3 Italian plum tomatoes, seeded
  and diced, optional

Process mint, garlic, nuts, salt and pepper in a food processor or blender until finely chopped and blended. While blender or processor is running, slowly add oil until blended and absorbed. Transfer mixture to a large bowl and add remaining ingredients, mixing well. Use as a filling for stuffed pizza or calzones.

Nutritional analysis per 1/8 recipe without dough 212 calories, 18.2 g fat, 11.2 g protein, 1.9 g carbohydrate, 38.2 mg cholesterol, 237 mg sodium

BROCCOLI AND CHEESE STUFFING

*This is absolutely superb with **Caraway Pepper Deep Dish Dough**, page 84. The 2 cups of broccoli is an estimation — more or less may be used. A 10 oz. package of frozen florets, cooked, may be used if fresh broccoli is unavailable.*

2 cups cooked, chopped broccoli florets
1½ cups grated mozzarella cheese
½ cup grated cheddar cheese
salt and pepper to taste
1 tsp. caraway seed, optional

Cook broccoli until just tender. In a large bowl mix together cooked broccoli and remaining ingredients. Use as a filling for stuffed pizza (see page 95) or calzones (see page 93).

Nutritional analysis per ⅛ ***recipe without dough*** *152 calories, 10.6 g fat, 12.2 g protein, 2.4 g carbohydrate, 35.2 mg cholesterol, 311 mg sodium*

SPINACH FILLING WITH FETA AND MOZZARELLA

*A delightful treat with **Lemon Pepper Deep Dish Dough**, page 86, or any herb deep dish dough.*

1 tbs. olive oil
1/4-1/3 cup diced red onion
1-2 cloves garlic minced or pressed
1 pkg. (10 oz.) frozen spinach,
  thawed and drained
2 oz. feta cheese
1/2 cup grated or shredded mozzarella cheese
1/4 cup freshly grated Parmesan cheese
1/4 cup pine nuts or chopped walnuts
1/2 tsp. grated lemon peel
1 tsp. dried mint or 1 tbs. chopped fresh
1/4-1/3 cup pizza sauce

Heat oil in large skillet over medium heat. Add onion and garlic and sauté until soft. Add spinach and sauté until heated through. Remove from heat and drain as much liquid as possible. Mix in remaining ingredients and set aside. Divide deep dish pizza dough recipe into two sections, one of which is about ⅔ the total amount with the remaining ⅓ to be set aside. Roll larger section of dough into a 14-inch circle and place in a greased 12-inch deep dish pizza pan with edges hanging over. Spread spinach mixture evenly over dough. Roll out remaining piece of pizza dough and place over pizza mixture. Fold edges over on top and seal with fingers. If desired, lightly brush the top with olive oil. Poke the top with a fork in 2 or 3 places to allow steam to escape. Bake in a preheated 450° oven for 20 to 30 minutes or until done.

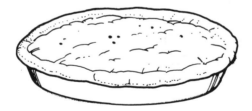

Nutritional analysis per ⅛ recipe without dough   102 calories, 7.4 g fat, 5.5 g protein, 4.6 g carbohydrate, 12.4 mg cholesterol, 294 mg sodium

PIZZA SAUCES AND TOPPINGS

BASIC PIZZA SAUCE

*This recipe makes approximately 2 cups of sauce, which is enough for several pizzas. Use what you need and refrigerate or freeze the rest in ½-cup amounts for quick and easy thawing later. Feel free to experiment with seasonings - it is **your** pizza after all!*

6-8 fresh Italian plum tomatoes, or 1
   can (28 oz.) of Italian plum tomatoes,
   rinsed and drained
1 clove garlic minced or pressed
2 tsp. dried oregano, or 2 tbs. fresh

1 tsp. dried basil, or 1 tbs. fresh
¼ tsp. cayenne, or ½ tsp. crushed red
   pepper flakes, optional
salt and pepper to taste

Seed tomatoes by cutting off stem top and squeezing them over a bowl or sink to remove seeds and juice. Process tomatoes in a blender or food processor (steel blade) for just a moment to chop coarsely. Tomatoes may also be chopped by hand if desired. Add herbs and seasonings to taste. If using right away, it need not be cooked; however, if it will be refrigerated or frozen, simmer sauce over low heat for 5 to 10 minutes. Sauce may be refrigerated in a tightly sealed container and used within a week or two.

Nutritional analysis per ⅛ recipe without dough   *26 calories, 0.4 g fat, 1.2 g protein, 5.8 g carbohydrate, 0 mg cholesterol, 10.3 mg sodium*

FENNEL PIZZA SAUCE

Fresh fennel is a common ingredient in Italian cooking. The bulbous part is diced and sautéed for added flavor in this pizza sauce. This recipe makes 1½ cups.

1 tbs. olive oil
¼ cup pine nuts
½ medium fennel bulb, diced
¼ medium red onion, diced
1-2 cloves garlic, minced or pressed
1 can (14.5 oz.) crushed tomatoes, drained

Heat oil in a large skillet, add nuts and cook over low heat for 1 to 2 minutes, stirring frequently. Add fennel, onion and garlic and cook until soft and tender. Add tomatoes and seasonings to taste. Simmer for about 5 minutes.

Nutritional analysis per ⅛ recipe without dough   *74 calories, 5.5 g fat, 2.3 g protein, 6 g carbohydrate, 0.0 mg cholestterol, 14.9 mg sodium*

GARDEN PIZZA SAUCE

This is a wonderful twist to a plain pizza sauce. It uses all those vegetables from your garden or when they are inexpensive in the stores. Make lots so you can freeze for later use.

½ zucchini, cut into chunks
2-3 Italian tomatoes, seeded, cut into chunks
¼ cup chopped onion
basil, salt and pepper to taste

Combine zucchini, tomatoes and onion in a food processor or blender and puree. Remove to a small saucepan, add seasonings to taste and simmer over low heat for 5 minutes.

Nutritional analysis per ⅛ *recipe without dough*   *12 calories, 0.1 g fat, 0.6 g protein, 2.7 g carbohydrate, 0 mg cholesterol, 4.5 mg sodium*

PESTO SAUCE AND TOPPING

It is imperative to use fresh herbs for pesto. Many stores carry pesto in the gourmet cheese section if you don't feel like making it! Fresh cilantro may be substituted for the basil but add crushed red pepper flakes to taste. Makes 1¾ cups.

SAUCE

1 cup fresh basil leaves, tightly packed
2-3 cloves garlic
¼ cup pine nuts or walnuts

salt and coarsely ground black pepper
  to taste
¼ cup olive oil
¼ cup freshly grated Parmesan cheese

TOPPING

1-1½ cups grated mozzarella cheese
freshly sliced Italian plum tomatoes, seeded and diced, optional

Process basil, garlic, nuts, salt and pepper in a food processor or blender until finely chopped and blended. While blender or processor is running, slowly add oil until blended and absorbed. Mix in Parmesan cheese until just blended. Spread pesto over pizza and top with cheese and tomatoes.

Nutritional analysis per ⅛ *recipe with toppings, without dough*   *109 calories, 10.1 g fat, 3.1 g protein, 6.3 g carbohydrate, 2.0 mg cholesterol, 194 mg sodium*

INDIAN PIZZA SAUCE AND TOPPING

*This recipe makes enough sauce for two 15-inch pizzas. Use what you need, and freeze or refrigerate unused portion for later use. Serve on **Ginger Pizza Dough**, page 65, or **Scallion Pizza Dough**, page 46. If a meat is desired, use finely diced cooked chicken, or ground lamb or beef, cooked, drained and crumbled.*

SAUCE
1 can (14.5 oz.) whole tomatoes,
  rinsed, drained and chopped
1/4 tsp. crushed red pepper flakes
2 tbs.-1/4 cup chopped onion
1/2 small zucchini, grated
2 cloves garlic, minced or pressed
1/2 tsp. cumin
1/4 tsp. coriander seed
1 tsp. curry
1 tbs. chopped ginger root or
  1 tsp. ground ginger
salt and pepper to taste

TOPPING

1 tbs. olive oil
½ cup plain yogurt
⅓-½ cup sauce, above
⅓-½ lb. deveined, cooked, diced shrimp,
  or ½ cup cooked, diced chicken
1 green or red bell pepper, thinly sliced
cilantro or parsley to taste

In a medium saucepan, mix together sauce ingredients and simmer over low heat for 5 minutes or until just warm; set aside. Lightly brush olive oil over dough and layer sauce and remaining topping ingredients in the order given.

Nutritional analysis per ⅛ recipe with topping, without dough 50 calories, 2.2 g fat, 5.0 g protein, 3.7 g carbohydrate, 28.8 mg cholesterol, 166 mg sodium

CHEESE TOPPING

This is a "must try" for anyone who ever asks for extra cheese! There is no pizza sauce but you could, of course, add some if you want. With this high amount of cheese, no other toppings should be used to prevent a soggy, uncooked middle. This same combination could also be used as a filling for a stuffed pizza or calzones.

1 tbs. olive oil
½ cup ricotta cheese
1 cup grated mozzarella cheese
½ cup grated Monterey Jack cheese
½ cup grated provolone cheese
¼ cup freshly grated Parmesan and/or
  Romano cheese

Lightly brush olive oil on dough. Spread ricotta on top and layer remaining cheese so there is less cheese in center of pizza. As the pizza cooks, the cheese will gravitate to the center.

Nutritional analysis per ⅛ recipe without dough   *118 calories, 8.9 g fat, 8.4 g protein, 1.1 g carbohydrate, 23.0 mg cholesterol, 183 mg sodium*

SEAFOOD SPECIAL TOPPING

*What a delightful treat! Use scallops (cooked), shrimp (cleaned and cooked), crab or a combination. Use **Garlic Herb Dough**, page 53 or 85 or **Lemon Pepper Dough,** page 44 or 86. Vegetables such as snow peas or broccoli can be added for a little extra crunch and flavor.*

4 oz. or $\frac{1}{2}$ cup cream cheese, optional
$\frac{1}{4}$-$\frac{1}{3}$ cup cocktail sauce
1 clove garlic, minced or pressed
Tabasco Sauce or peppers to taste, optional
$\frac{1}{2}$ lb. seafood, cut into bite-size chunks
1-2 green onions (scallions), diced or
  $\frac{1}{4}$ cup diced red onions
1-2 cups grated mozzarella cheese
lemon peel to taste, optional

If using cream cheese, spread it over the pizza dough, leaving a $\frac{1}{2}$-inch border. Spread cocktail sauce on top and layer remaining ingredients in the order given.

Nutritional analysis per $\frac{1}{8}$ recipe without dough   54 calories, 1.7 g fat, 7.9 g protein, 2.6 g carbohydrate, 47.0 mg cholesterol, 173 mg sodium

CRAB TOPPING

*Serve this outstanding pizza on **Lemon Pepper Dough**, page 44 or 86, **Parsley Pepper Dough**, page 49 or 89 or **Garlic Cheese Thin Crust Dough**, page 58. A great appetizer pizza! Fresh crab is best but if using frozen, thaw and drain it well.*

4 oz. or ½ cup softened cream cheese
1 tsp. lemon juice
1 tsp. lemon pepper
½ tsp. horseradish
salt to taste

¼ cup diced red onion
½ cup flaked or chunked crab meat
1-1½ cups grated mozzarella cheese
¼ cup chopped almonds
parsley to taste

Mix together cream cheese, lemon juice, lemon pepper, horseradish and salt. Spread over dough, leaving a ½-inch border around the edge. Layer remaining ingredients in order given.

Nutritional analysis per ⅛ recipe without dough 135 calories, 8.5 g fat, 12.0 g protein, 2.5 g carbohydrate, 45.2 mg cholesterol, 396 mg sodium

SHRIMP FETA TOPPING

*Serve this with **Cilantro Thin Crust Dough**, page 57 or **Mint Thin Crust Dough**, page 50. Any of your favorite (precooked) vegetables such as broccoli, snow peas or asparagus could be added to this for flavor and color.*

1 tbs. olive oil, optional
2-3 oz. or ½ cup crumbled feta cheese
⅓-½ lb. cooked shrimp, peeled and diced
1-2 cups grated mozzarella cheese
fresh or dried cilantro, basil or mint to taste

Lightly brush dough with olive oil. Top with cheese, shrimp and herbs to taste.

Nutritional analysis per ⅛ recipe without dough   *75 calories, 4.3 g fat, 8.8 g protein, 1.0 g carbohydrate, 42.6 mg cholesterol, 180 mg sodium*

SCALLOP TOPPING

*Bay scallops are small and tender and do not need to be cut into small pieces. Serve on **Scallion Thin Crust Dough**, page 46, or **Lemon Pepper Dough**, page 44 or 86.*

1 tbs. olive oil
½ tsp. lemon juice
⅓-½ lb. scallops, bite sized
¼-⅓ cup ricotta cheese
¼ cup bacon, cooked, drained and crumbled

1-2 green onion (scallion), diced white and green part
½-1 green bell pepper, diced or sliced
1-2 cups grated mozzarella cheese
thyme to taste

Sauté scallops in olive oil and lemon juice for about 5 minutes for bay scallops or 8 minutes for sea scallops. Remove from heat and drain scallops, reserving oil, and set aside. Lightly brush oil over pizza dough. Layer scallops and remaining ingredients. Season to taste.

Nutritional analysis per ⅛ recipe without dough 89 calories, 5.4 g fat, 8.3 g protein, 1.6 g carbohydrate, 18.8 mg cholesterol, 134 mg sodium

HAWAIIAN TOPPING

*This is superb with **Pineapple Thin Crust Dough**, page 43. Cooked, diced turkey or chicken may be substituted for the ham.*

¼-⅓ cup pizza sauce
1 can (8 oz.) pineapple chunks, drained
½ cup diced ham
¼ cup diced or sliced red onion
½ cup grated provolone cheese
1-1½ cups grated mozzarella cheese

Spread just enough pizza sauce to cover pizza dough, leaving a ½- to 1-inch border around the rim. Layer remaining ingredients in the order given.

Nutritional analysis per ⅛ recipe without dough 113 calories, 4.8 g fat, 7.9 g protein, 10.1 g carbohydrate, 15.0 mg cholesterol, 281 mg sodium

ORANGE CHICKEN TOPPING

*Serve this with **Orange Poppy Seed Thin Crust Dough**, page 42 or **Orange Ginger Thin Crust Dough**, page 45. Up to ½ cup of the mozzarella may be replaced with feta.*

1 tbs. olive oil, optional
¼-⅓ cup pizza sauce
½ cup diced cooked chicken
1 can (15 oz.) mandarin orange
  segments, drained and rinsed
1-2 cups grated mozzarella cheese

Lightly brush dough with olive oil. Spread just enough pizza sauce to cover pizza dough, leaving a ½- to 1-inch border around the rim. Spread chicken (or turkey) and orange segments evenly over pizza and top with grated cheese. Season with salt, pepper and/or orange peel.

Nutritional analysis per ⅛ recipe withhout dough 90 calories, 3.1 g fat, 7.2 g protein, 8.4 g carbohydrate, 15.5 mg cholesterol, 127 mg sodium

CRAN CHICKEN TOPPING

*There is something magical about the combination of cranberries and chicken, and it is no exception on pizza. Use any flavor of the **Cran Fruit**™ by Ocean Spray. I like the cranberry orange flavor. Any leftover turkey or chicken could be used. This is great with **Orange Ginger Thin Crust Dough**, page 45. If using a different flavor of **Cran Fruit**™, you may wish to use a different fruit in place of the orange segments.*

⅓ - ½ cup *Cran Fruit*™
½ cup cooked diced chicken
½ cup mandarin orange segments
1-2 cups grated mozzarella cheese
¼ cup chopped almonds, optional

Spread just enough *Cran Fruit*™ to cover pizza dough, leaving a ½-inch border. Layer chicken, orange segments and cheese on top. Sprinkle with almonds if desired.

Nutritional analysis per ⅛ recipe *105 calories, 5.9 g fat, 6.1 g protein, 6.6 g carbohydrate, 19 mg cholesterol, 61.5 mg sodium*

CHICKEN BBQ TOPPING

Add any and all of your favorite pizza toppings to this, such as red onions, green bell peppers, etc. As a variation, try grated fontina and smoked gouda instead of the basic mozzarella.

1 tbs. olive oil, optional
$1/4$-$1/3$ cup favorite barbecue sauce
$1/2$ cup diced cooked chicken
  (barbecued or simply microwaved)
1-$1^1/2$ cups grated mozzarella cheese
$1/2$ cup grated Fontina cheese, optional

$1/2$ cup grated smoked gouda cheese,
  optional
$1/4$ cup sliced or diced red onions
$1/2$-1 green bell pepper, sliced or diced
oregano and/or basil to taste

Lightly spread pizza dough with 1 tbs. olive oil if desired. Spread just enough sauce to cover pizza dough leaving a $1/2$-inch border around the rim. Layer remaining ingredients.

Nutritional analysis per $1/8$ recipe without dough 65 calories, 3.2 g fat, 6.7 g protein, 2.2 g carbohydrate, 15.5 mg cholesterol, 145 mg sodium

TERIYAKI CHICKEN TOPPING

*Use plain teriyaki sauce or your favorite teriyaki marinade (homemade or commercially prepared) for this. Serve with **Ginger Thin Crust Dough**, page 65 or **Garlic Cheese Thin Crust Dough**, page 58. A basic pizza sauce may be used in place of or in addition to the olive oil, but I like it without the tomato taste.*

¼ cup teriyaki sauce or marinade
1 boneless chicken breast, cut into
 ½-inch cubes
1 tbs. olive oil
1 can (8 oz.) pineapple chunks
½ cup crumbled feta cheese

1-1½ cup grated mozzarella cheese
ground ginger to taste, optional
crushed red pepper flakes to taste,
 optional
toasted sesame seeds, optional

Place chicken in a glass or plastic bowl and pour marinade over top. Refrigerate for 2 to 3 hours. Cook chicken on a grill, in an oiled skillet or in the microwave. This may be done in advance if desired. Lightly brush olive oil on dough, spread cooked chicken on top and layer all remaining ingredients in the order given.

Nutritional analysis per ⅛ recipe without dough *129 calories, 6.1 g fat, 10.0 g protein, 6.4 g carbohydrate, 30.8 mg cholesterol, 517 mg sodium*

CHICKEN FETA TOPPING

A basic throw-together pizza using any and all of your favorite pizza toppings. This does not call for a pizza sauce, but one could be used if desired.

1 tbs. olive oil
½ cup diced cooked chicken (1 breast)
2-3 oz. or ½ cup feta cheese, crumbled
1-1½ cups grated mozzarella cheese
green bell pepper, diced or sliced, to taste
red onion, diced or sliced, to taste
2-3 Italian plum tomatoes, seeded and sliced
basil, mint and/or oregano to taste

Lightly brush dough with olive oil. Layer remaining ingredients in order given. Season with fresh or dried herbs to taste.

Nutritional analysis per ⅛ recipe without dough 120 calories, 6.1 g fat, 9.7 g protein, 4.3 g carbohydrate, 30.8 mg cholesterol, 174 mg sodium

CHICKEN GRUYÈRE TOPPING

*This is great with **Basic Garlic Thin Crust Dough**, page 60, or **Scallion Thin Crust Dough**, page 46. I like to use an olive oil with garlic in it for a little extra flavor.*

1 tbs. olive oil
½ cup cooked chicken or turkey, diced
1-1½ cups shredded Gruyère cheese
diced Tabasco Sauce or
  jalapeño peppers to taste
1 green onion (scallion), diced, or
  ¼ cup diced red onion
cumin to taste

Lightly brush dough with olive oil. Layer remaining ingredients in the order given.

Nutritional analysis per** ⅛ **recipe without dough   *74 calories, 3.5 g fat, 6.5 g protein, 1.2 g carbohydrate 32.5 mg cholesterol, 157 mg sodium*

ASIAN CHICKEN TOPPING

*Serve this with **Anise Thin Crust Dough**, page 63 (variation of Fennel Dough), or **Orange Ginger Thin Crust Dough**, page 45.*

¼ cup soy sauce
1 tbs. sesame oil
½ tsp. crushed red pepper flakes
1 tbs. freshly grated ginger or ½ tsp.
  powder
1 tsp. anise seed
½ cup diced cooked chicken
1 can (8 oz.) pineapple chunks, drained

¼ cup grated carrots
¼ cup sliced mushrooms, sliced,
  optional
½ green onion, sliced or diced, optional
1-2 cups grated mozzarella cheese
chopped fresh mint or dried mint to
  taste

Combine soy sauce, sesame oil, red pepper flakes, ginger and anise together and lightly brush over pizza dough. Layer remaining ingredients in the order given.

Nutritional analysis per ⅛ recipe without dough 68 calories, 3.2 g fat, 4.3 g protein, 5.7 g carbohydrate, 10.7 mg cholesterol, 546 mg sodium

LEBANESE TOPPING

Cinnamon Thin Crust Dough, *page 56, is a great crust for this flavorful, easy pizza.*

1 tbs. olive oil, optional
¼-⅓ cup pizza sauce
2-3 oz. or ½ cup feta cheese
1-1½ cups grated mozzarella cheese
½ cup ground beef, turkey or lamb,
  cooked, drained and crumbled

¼ cup onion, diced or sliced
¼ tsp. black pepper or to taste
½ tsp. cinnamon
1 tsp. dried basil or 1 tbs. chopped fresh
¼ cup pine nuts or chopped walnuts

Lightly spread pizza dough with olive oil if desired. Spread just enough pizza sauce to cover pizza dough, leaving a ½- to 1-inch border around the rim. Layer cheese, meat and onion. Season to taste and sprinkle with nuts.

Nutritional analysis per ⅛ recipe without dough 117 calories, 8.6 g fat, 8.1 g protein, 2.3 g carbohydrate, 29.2 mg cholesterol, 193 mg sodium

LAMB PIZZA

*Serve this treat on **Spinach Dough**, page 40 or 80, or **Lemon Pepper Dough**, page 44 or 86.*

1 tbs. olive oil, optional
½ cup cooked ground lamb,
  drained and crumbled
2-3 oz. or ½ cup crumbled feta cheese
1-1½ cups grated mozzarella cheese
2-3 tbs. pine nuts, optional
sliced pimientos and/or jalapeños
  to taste, optional

Lightly brush oil on dough. Layer remaining ingredients in the order given.

Nutritional analysis per ⅛ recipe without dough   *109 calories, 9.3 g fat, 6.0 g protein, 6.6 g carbohydrate, 26.9 mg cholesterol, 159 mg sodium*

FRUIT TOPPING

*Use a sweet dough, such as **Orange Poppy Seed Thin Crust Dough**, page 42, or **Sweet Thin Crust Dough**, page 34, for this delectable treat. If a richer, creamier cheese is desired, replace half of the ricotta with softened cream cheese. Red grapes, cut in half, may be added also.*

1 cup ricotta cheese
1 tsp. orange peel
1 pint strawberries, sliced
honey or maple syrup

Prebake pizza dough in a 350° oven for 5 minutes or until crust is brown. Mix together ricotta and orange peel and spread over dough, leaving a ½-inch border. Layer the strawberries on cheese, drizzle honey lightly on top and bake for 10 minutes.

Nutritional analysis per ⅛ ***recipe without dough*** *74 calories, 4.1 g fat, 3.7 g protein, 6.0 g carbohydrate, 15.8 mg cholesterol, 38.8 mg sodium*

PEACH BREAKFAST TOPPING

*A wonderful dessert or brunch treat. Use **Sweet Thin Crust Dough**, page 34. The initial reaction when you place this in front of someone will probably be something like, "They have lost their minds - a peach pizza?" But, once it is tasted, you'll have them asking for more.*

1-2 tbs. honey
2/3-3/4 cup almonds
2 tbs. sugar
3-4 fresh peaches, sliced, or
   equivalent canned, rinsed

Preheat oven to 375°. Brush dough lightly with just enough honey to cover the top. Process almonds in a blender or food processor (steel blade) until finely ground into a coarse meal. Do not over-blend or process. Blend sugar into almonds and spread mixture over crust. Top with sliced peaches and bake for 30 minutes or until the crust is brown.

Nutritional analysis per 1/8 recipe without dough 114 calories, 6.6 g fat, 2.4 g protein, 13.1 g carbohydrate, 0 mg cholesterol, 76.7 mg sodium

BREAKFAST TOPPING

Combine any of your favorite omelet toppings following these simple guidelines. If serving an early breakfast, prepare the dough the evening before, place in a plastic bag in the refrigerator (sealed, but leave room for the dough to expand) and roll it out in the morning. This easy, but fancy, breakfast will have house guests impressed!

¼-½ cup ricotta cheese
2-3 eggs, beaten
seasonings such as salt, pepper,
  nutmeg, basil, etc. to taste

¼-⅓ cup toppings: bacon, sausage,
  ham (meats should be precooked and
  sliced or crumbled), grated cheeses,
  diced vegetables, optional

Roll dough and crimp edges to form a high rim to hold uncooked egg in place. If you want a crispy crust, bake the shell only for about 5 minutes prior to topping it. If you want a chewy crust, do not prebake it. Spread ricotta cheese evenly on top of pizza dough, leaving a ½-inch border. Beat eggs with seasonings and pour on top of cheese (2 large eggs for a 10-inch thin crust pizza, 3 large eggs for 15-inch). Do not overfill with eggs. Place toppings on pizza so that there is less in the center than around the edges. Bake in a preheated 350° oven for 15 to 20 minutes.

Nutritional analysis per ⅛ recipe without dough or toppings   *46 calories, 3.3 g fat, 3.3 g protein, 0.7 g carbohydrate, 61.1 mg cholesterol, 28.8 mg sodium*

BRIE WITH ALMOND TOPPING

*This is a wonderful, sweet topping for **Flaky Deep Dish Dough**, page 91, or **Sweet Thin Crust Dough**, page 34. Slivered almonds may be used instead of the finely chopped — use about ³⁄₄ cup.*

3 tbs. melted butter or margarine
¹⁄₂ cup finely chopped almonds
2 tbs. brown sugar
slices of Brie cheese to cover

Mix butter, almonds and brown sugar together and spread over dough. Layer Brie slices decoratively.

Nutritional analysis per ¹⁄₈ recipe   148 calories, 12.5 g fat, 4.3 g protein, 5.5 g carbohydrate, 14 mg cholesterol, 196 mg sodium

APPLE PIE TOPPING

*Serve this on **Cinnamon Thin Crust Dough**, page 56, or **Flaky Deep Dish Dough**, page 91. Any of your favorite pie filling could be used. If serving as an appetizer or with brunch, try adding some cooked, crumbled sausage — sweet or Italian, depending on your mood.*

1 (20 oz.) can apple pie filling
½ cup grated cheddar cheese, optional
¼ cup chopped walnuts
¼ cup golden raisins, optional

Spread apple pie filling over dough. Cover with cheese if desired and sprinkle with nuts and raisins.

Nutritional analysis per ⅛ *recipe*   *242 calories, 10.2 g fat, 4.0 g protein, 35.7 g carbohydrate, 7.4 mg cholesterol, 262 mg sodium*

BLACK BEAN TOPPING

*Use your favorite salsa for this hot and spicy treat! Terrific with **Spicy Corn Thin Crust Dough**, page 66. I use canned beans for convenience, but make sure to rinse thoroughly to remove the salt.*

1 tbs. olive oil, optional
1/3 cup salsa
1 cup black beans, rinsed and drained
1 cup grated mozzarella cheese
1/2 cup grated Monterey Jack cheese
  with or without jalapeños
1/2 cup grated cheddar cheese
1/4 cup red onion, sliced or diced

1-2 cloves garlic, minced or pressed,
  optional
1/2-1 red or green bell pepper, diced or
  sliced, optional
jalapeño peppers, diced or sliced, to
  taste
crushed red pepper flakes to taste,
  optional
cilantro to taste, optional

Lightly spread pizza dough with olive oil if desired. Spread just enough salsa to cover pizza dough, leaving a 1/2-inch border around the rim. Layer remaining ingredients.

Nutritional analysis per** 1/8 **recipe without dough *154 calories, 9.5 g fat, 8.5 g protein, 7.5 g carbohydrate, 24.7 mg cholesterol, 353 mg sodium*

SOUTHWESTERN TOPPING

*Serve this on a cornmeal dough, pages 61, 66, or 83 or a **Mexican Herb Dough**, page 54 or 88. Canned corn kernels should be rinsed and drained well.*

1/4-1/3 cup salsa
1 cup grated Monterey Jack cheese
1 cup grated mozzarella cheese
1/2 cup corn kernels
1 green onion (scallion), julienned or diced
chili powder or cumin to taste

Spread salsa evenly on top of dough, leaving a 1/2-inch border. Top with cheese, corn and onion. Season to taste.

Nutritional analysis per 1/8 recipe without dough   107 calories, 7.5 g fat, 6.6 g protein, 3.2 g carbohydrate, 23.5 mg cholesterol, 213 mg sodium

MACHO NACHO TOPPING

If you like nachos, try this pizza. Serve with any of the corn, Mexican or hot and spicy pizza doughs. Feel free to improvise according to your taste buds and what's sitting in the refrigerator! Cooked, diced chicken, ground meat with a taco sauce or peeled shrimp could be added to this as well. Of course, you can go the other way and have nothing but salsa and cheese. Top with a dollop of sour cream and/or guacamole after cooking.

$\frac{1}{2}$ cup refried beans
$\frac{1}{4}$-$\frac{1}{3}$ cup salsa
$\frac{1}{2}$ cup grated cheddar cheese
$\frac{1}{2}$ cup grated Monterey Jack cheese
   with or without jalapeños
1 cup grated mozzarella cheese
2 scallions (green onions) diced or
   $\frac{1}{4}$ cup diced red onion
jalapeño peppers, sliced to taste
crushed red pepper flakes to taste

Nutritional analysis per $\frac{1}{8}$ recipe without dough   113 calories, 7.6 g fat, 7.3 g protein, 3.5 g carbohydrate, 24.7 mg cholesterol, 222 mg sodium

BRAZILIAN LEMON PEPPER TOPPING

This is an adaptation of a sauce which is normally served with feijoada, the national black bean dish. Use this as a topping with **Black Bean Thin Crust Dough**, *page 47. Jalapeños may be substituted for the Tabasco peppers. If meat is desired, use diced, cooked shrimp or poultry.*

1 tbs. olive oil
2 tbs. lemon juice
1-2 cups grated mozzarella cheese
4-5 pickled Tabasco peppers,
  finely chopped (bottled)
$\frac{1}{4}$ medium onion, finely chopped
1-2 cloves garlic, minced or pressed
$\frac{1}{4}$ cup fresh parsley, chopped or
  1 tbs. dried

Mix olive oil and lemon juice together and spread over pizza dough. Top with remaining ingredients in order given and bake.

Nutritional analysis per $\frac{1}{8}$ *recipe without dough*   60 calories, 4.9 g fat, 3.2 g protein, 2.5 g carbohydrate, 11.0 mg cholesterol, 75 mg sodium

FENNEL TOPPING

*Fresh fennel is a real treat when you can find it. The whole bulb is is used on pizza. Finely dice or chop by hand or process coarsely in a food processor (steel blade) so you have small chunks. Serve on **Fennel Thin Crust Dough**, page 63.*

1 tbs. olive oil
½ medium fennel bulb, diced
¼ medium red onion, diced
1-2 cloves garlic, minced or pressed
¼-⅓ cup pizza sauce or salsa
1-1½ cups grated mozzarella
¼ cup freshly grated Parmesan cheese
fennel seeds to taste, optional

Heat oil in large skillet, add fennel, onion and garlic and cook until soft and tender. Set aside. Spread sauce on crust, leaving a ½-inch border. Spread fennel mixture over sauce and top with cheeses.

Nutritional analysis per ⅛ *recipe without dough*   *71 calories, 5.6 g fat, 3.9 g protein, 1.1 g carbohydrate, 13.0 mg cholesterol, 183 mg sodium*

VEGETABLE TOPPING

*A must for an overflowing garden. Serve on **Tomato Basil Thin Crust Dough**, page 52, **Three Pepper Dough**, page 51 or 90, or **Basic Garlic Thin Crust Dough**, page 60.*

1 tbs. olive oil
2-3 small summer squash and/or
  zucchini squash, sliced or diced
½ medium red onion, diced or sliced
1-2 garlic cloves, minced or pressed

1 red or green bell pepper, sliced or
  diced, optional
1-2 cups grated mozzarella cheese
basil, cilantro or oregano to taste
crushed red pepper flakes

Heat oil in a large skillet. Add vegetables and sauté lightly until just soft. Spread mixture on top of pizza dough leaving a ½- to 1-inch border. Top with cheese and season to taste using herbs of choice, fresh or dried.

Nutritional analysis per ⅛ *recipe without dough*   *62 calories, 4.9 g fat, 3.2 g protein, 2.0 g carbohydrate, 11.0 mg cholesterol, 54.3 mg sodium*

NO SAUCE TOMATO TOPPING

When your garden is overflowing (or the tomatoes are ripe and cheap at the store) it can be very gratifying to use fresh tomatoes on your pizza. This is a very simple and basic pizza which has become one of my favorites. While I do not usually add the mozzarella, some taste testers prefer it.

1 tbs. olive oil
3-4 Italian plum tomatoes, seeded and diced
3-4 oz. or heaping ½ cup feta cheese, crumbled
1 cup grated mozzarella, optional
oregano, basil or mint to taste

Lightly brush olive oil over crust of pizza. Layer tomatoes and cheese on top and season with fresh or dried herbs.

Nutritional analysis per ⅛ recipe without dough   47 calories, 4.1 g fat, 1.9 g protein, 1.3 g carbohydrate, 9.4 mg cholesterol, 1.9 mg sodium

SPINACH TOPPING

*This may be served on **Lemon Pepper Dough**, page 44 or 86, **Mint Thin Crust Dough**, page 50 or **Spinach Dough**, page 40 or 80. One 10 oz. box of frozen chopped spinach, well drained and patted dry, equals about 1 cup.*

1 tbs. olive oil
1-2 cloves garlic, minced or pressed
1/4 cup diced red onion
1 cup fresh spinach, chopped and tightly packed
1/2 cup ricotta cheese
2-3 oz. or 1/2 cup feta cheese, crumbled
1 cup grated mozzarella cheese

Heat oil in a large skillet. Add garlic, onion, and spinach and sauté until onion is soft and spinach is just wilted. Remove from heat and stir in ricotta cheese. Spread mixture over dough, leaving a 1/2- to 1-inch border. Layer remaining cheeses.

Nutritional analysis per** 1/8 **recipe without dough *117 calories, 9.2 g fat, 6.9 g protein, 2.5 g carbohydrate, 28.3 mg cholesterol, 199 mg sodium*

BROCCOLI TOPPING

*You can always throw broccoli on a pizza with nothing more than pizza sauce and mozzarella, but this is better! Pizza sauce may be used if desired. Serve with any pizza dough or with **Fennel Thin Crust Dough** using caraway seeds, page 63.*

1 tbs. olive oil
1/2 cup grated cheddar cheese
1-1 1/2 cups grated mozzarella cheese
1 cup broccoli florets, cooked until
  just tender

2-3 Italian plum tomatoes, seeded
  and diced
1/4 cup red onion, diced or sliced
caraway seeds, or crushed red pepper
  flakes to taste

Lightly brush dough with olive oil. Layer remaining ingredients in the order given. Season to taste.

VARIATION

- **BACON, CHEDDAR AND BROCCOLI TOPPING:** Omit tomatoes, onion and caraway seeds and add 1/2 cup cooked, crumbled bacon.

Nutritional analysis per 1/8 recipe without dough   90.3 calories, 7.2 g fat, 5.0 g protein, 2.0 g carbohydrate, 18.4 mg cholesterol, 101 mg sodium
Variation per 1/8 recipe without dough   64 calories, 5.3 g fat, 3.6 g protein, 0.6 g carbohydrate, 12.6 mg cholesterol, 102 mg sodium

INDEX

SERVE CREATIVE, EASY, NUTRITIOUS MEALS WITH NITTY GRITTY® COOKBOOKS

The Best Bagels are made at home
The Toaster Oven Cookbook
Skewer Cooking on the Grill
Creative Mexican Cooking
Extra-Special Crockery Pot Recipes
Cooking in Clay
Marinades
Deep Fried Indulgences
Cooking with Parchment Paper
The Garlic Cookbook
Flatbreads From Around the World
From Your Ice Cream Maker
Favorite Cookie Recipes
Cappuccino/Espresso: The Book of
  Beverages
Indoor Grilling
Slow Cooking
The Best Pizza is made at home
The Well Dressed Potato
Convection Oven Cookery

The Steamer Cookbook
The Pasta Machine Cookbook
The Versatile Rice Cooker
The Dehydrator Cookbook
The Bread Machine Cookbook
The Bread Machine Cookbook II
The Bread Machine Cookbook III
The Bread Machine Cookbook IV
The Bread Machine Cookbook V
The Bread Machine Cookbook VI
Worldwide Sourdoughs From Your
  Bread Machine
Recipes for the Pressure Cooker
The New Blender Book
The Sandwich Maker Cookbook
Waffles
The Coffee Book
The Juicer Book
The Juicer Book II
Bread Baking (traditional)
The Kid's Cookbook

No Salt, No Sugar, No Fat
  Cookbook
Cooking for 1 or 2
Quick and Easy Pasta Recipes
The 9x13 Pan Cookbook
Extra-Special Crockery Pot Recipes
Chocolate Cherry Tortes and
  Other Lowfat Delights
Low Fat American Favorites
Now That's Italian!
Fabulous Fiber Cookery
Low Salt, Low Sugar, Low Fat
  Desserts
Healthy Cooking on the Run
Healthy Snacks for Kids
Muffins, Nut Breads and More
The Wok
New Ways to Enjoy Chicken
Favorite Seafood Recipes
New International Fondue Cookbook

For a free catalog, write or call:
Bristol Publishing Enterprises, Inc.
P.O. Box 1737
San Leandro, CA 94577
(800) 346-4889; in California, (510) 895-4461